WIDOW'S WALK

WIDOW'S WALK

Anne Hosansky

DONALD I. FINE, INC.
New York

ACKNOWLEDGMENTS

IF NO ONE is an "island" (apologies to Donne for unisexing his famed line), that's triply true for writers. This book wasn't created in a vacuum; many wonderful people helped to light the way. I am deeply indebted to:

- Donald I. Fine, my publisher, for being committed to this book and for his insightful comments.

- Mildred Marmur—the most dedicated agent any author could be blessed with—for believing in this work from the beginning.

- Sarah Gallick, the perceptive editor who brought this book to·Donald Fine's attention.

- The members of my writing workshop, for their patience in listening to excerpts week after week, and for their superlative critiques, I thank Carol Emshwiller, Robert Fagan, Joanna Torrey and Peter Bricklebank.

• My sisters and brothers in the support groups, who openly shared their feelings. And Annette Brick and Dominick Bonanno of Cancer Care, who contributed valuable insights.

• The many generous friends who constitute an ongoing cheering section. It's almost unfair to single out anyone, but I do want to pay special tribute to Eleanor and Stanley Hochman, who translated their regard for me into action by recommending me to Milly Marmur. Affectionate thanks also go to Dorothy and Charles Weinberg, Edie and Chuck Morse, Yvonne Middleton, Hollis Cohen and Judith Bristol for all the encouraging words. And I'm grateful to my sister, Sonia Boin, for nurturance during the darkest days.

• Verbal hugs to my children, Tamar and David, for their loving supportiveness. And thanks, Pat Sparling, for echoing their enthusiasm.

• Last—but like Abou Ben Adhem leading all the rest— Mel, whose love and encouraging spirit were with me throughout the writing of our story.

A.H.

"Light One Candle," Chapter 22. Words and music by Peter Yarrow. ©1983 Silver Dawn Music, used by permission.

This is the story of one woman's walk through the first year and a half of widowhood. Certain names have been changed to protect privacy, but the experiences are true. It is my hope that sharing them may help you on your own journey toward survival.

FOR MEL

1

I'VE NEVER BEEN a widow before. It wasn't a role I cared to rehearse, even though I knew for twenty-three months that I was losing Mel.

But there's no way to be prepared for the things that hit you. You know that birthdays and anniversaries and holidays will be killers, but you don't expect this: On this ordinary day, reaching into the supermarket dairy case for a container of milk, you see the black lettering on it that reads EXPIRATION DATE JULY 16TH. You cry out. The carton falls from your hands. Milk pours over the floor. People are staring at you. The manager hurries over. "What's the problem, lady?"

How do you tell him the "expiration date" is your husband's birthday—and your husband has just died?

Nobody warns you about the "slide shows," either. That's what my bereavement group calls the constant reruns. You're riding on a bus or walking down the street or lying in bed, but scenes keep replaying. I'm seeing Mel in the hospital, slumped over in a chair while I help the nurse bathe the skin that's so paper-thin the bones hurt my palms. Or we're at the dinner table. I'm urging him to eat, he's angry that I keep trying. "Why the hell don't you give up?" he says.

Every time I get into bed, I see us lying here the night I broke down in front of him for the first time. "I don't want to be left," I cried like a baby. "I don't want to leave you," he said, putting his arms around me as though he thought he could keep us safe. But I was angry at myself for getting upset in front of him. He was so quick to pick up on my fear, like a virus he shouldn't be exposed to.

HE'D BEEN complaining about a "tight feeling" in his stomach. Nothing serious, he thought, probably tension because we were planning our first trip to Italy and he was anxiety-ridden about it (a travel editor who was always nervous about traveling!). But he agreed to see a doctor, who sent him for an abdominal CAT scan. Mel was away on a business trip when the call came. A matter-of-fact voice said he was the doctor, was my husband there? I said no, suddenly chilled, was there a message? He spoke the six words that started it: "Something's shown up on the liver."

I ran to the other extension to call a friend who'd had liver problems. I don't know why I went to the other phone. Maybe I felt it was farther away from that cool professional voice. My friend assured me "liver" could mean a lot of things that aren't necessarily fatal. Hepatitis, she said, maybe an inflammation. But I knew. Right from the beginning, I knew. As though dusk was settling into the room. I wondered what the world would be like without . . . But that couldn't be. We'd been married for thirty-seven years. He had been the center of my life since I was eighteen. Some things just can't be allowed to happen.

"YOU DON'T know how much I want this to be over," he's saying. I put my arm around his shoulder, so thin and sharp it appalls me to touch it.

That's what I'm replaying tonight. We were sitting on this couch. It's a long sectional, and it seems bigger when there's just one person. But I can see the two of us sitting at the other end.

"Will you try to have a Sustacal?" I'm asking for—what, the hundredth time? That's the liquid supplement that takes the place of the food he can't digest anymore. It comes in all kinds of colorful flavors, like the milk shakes he used to love. How tight my voice sounds, because I know that asking is the prelude to a battle. But he just says wearily, "All right."

"Strawberry or vanilla?" I recite again. He sits there with his head in his hands, not answering. It makes me feel like a murderer. And murderous. I pour strawberry Sustacal over ice, stir until the pink liquid froths up, put a straw in it, place the glass on the table in front of him.

"Please," I beg.

But he doesn't drink it.

What do you do with the guilt about the anger after it's all over?

"THE SUBJECT today is anger." I've joined a support group, and that's what the leader's announcing at my first meeting. It's as if she's thrown a dirty cloth on the table.

"How can we be angry?" one of the women says. "Our husbands didn't *want* to die."

We all nod. I'm seeing Mel the night he first began to think he might not live. "It's hard to part," he's saying, stroking my cheek.

I'm not angry, I keep telling myself. I go into a coffee shop and sit in a booth. The waitress says, "You can't have a booth if you're alone." I want to kill her. She tells me I have to move to one of the smaller tables. I refuse. And sit there choking on my English muffin, scalding my mouth with hot tea, sure that she and the other waitresses and the manager and the people walking past looking through the window are all mad that I'm taking up an entire booth just for me.

THIS IS what it means to be a widow these first months . . .

You get used to carrying buff-colored death certificates in your purse because you have to have them handy.

You're supposed to make a million decisions when you can't even decide if it's worthwhile to get out of bed in the morning.

You still close the door when you go to the bathroom because it isn't really possible you're the only one who's living in the apartment now.

You hate yourself for never trying to understand what he was talking about with those IRAs and CDs and municipal bonds and whatnots that you're supposed to add up, divide, transfer—and can't.

You don't notify American Express that the account should be in your name, because you're afraid that as an unemployed woman you won't be considered a good credit risk. Ditto the department stores. These are only some of the things you're afraid of as you try widowhood on for size.

This is what it also means: you're always on the run—like a fugitive—doing anything to avoid going home. Because home is where he *isn't*.

But wherever you run to, it has to be where you didn't go together.

Which means you can't walk into a movie theatre because that's the hand-holding thing you did on Saturday nights.

And you cross the street to avoid walking past the neighborhood Italian restaurant where you went for birthday dinners.

And all the scorching summer you don't go to the beach, because that's what you used to do on weekends (and before that, when you were young and falling in love, lying on a blanket with his sandy—healthy—body holding yours).

"Get on with your life." That's what people keep saying. You don't understand what the words mean. Maybe they mean you should stop running. So you try to stay in what used to be your home . . .

. . . Where magazines pile up on the coffee table, still in their mailing wrappers. You pick up the last opened copy of The New Yorker. It's dated February 19. He had nine days left. Were there cartoons that made him laugh?

. . . Where you turn on the TV and notice that all the commercials and movie clips show couples.

In the middle of the night you lie awake staring into the darkness, thinking you'll never again know love or sex.

But a part of you doesn't believe he isn't just on another business trip and that he won't call from some hotel to say, "Hi, honey, I miss you."

You think of all the times he went on those trips and how resentful you were at being "abandoned" for a few days, especially over a weekend. A *weekend*, for the love of God! We're talking about forever now.

You see a tall thin man carrying an attaché case walking double-time in that familiar way, and you hurry to catch up. But it's a stranger's face that turns toward you.

"It's always there." That's what your daughter says. You both know what she means. But she goes home each night to someone who loves her.

Your son says, "I felt bad yesterday, then I realized it was because it was a Wednesday." The day Mel died. You don't tell him that for you *every* day is Wednesday.

Your mother's vegetating in a nursing home. Ninety, a shell waiting to die. He was sixty-four and wanted to be allowed to live.

You're afraid to think that maybe you're angry at God.

2

I HAVE DIFFICULTY remembering the "B.C." days—Before Cancer. I'm unable to see Mel's face the way it was before it became so hollow-cheeked under an eerily bald skull. Can't hear his voice sounding eager, can't recall conversations that didn't constantly revolve around his illness. Around and around and around until I thought I would go mad. Sometimes I thought *anything* would be better, that afterwards at least I wouldn't have to listen to this all day, all night.

That goes in the Guilt Bag, too.

Our wedding photo is hanging on the bedroom wall. I can't look at it. One night, anesthetized by wine, I find myself standing in front of the picture, staring at that unrecognizable couple. Who is that young man wearing a mustache to make himself look older? He was younger than our son is now! And who is that girl with such hopeful eyes?

Last year, when Mel was so ill, I went on a frantic cleaning streak. (If you clean up the closets and bureau drawers, you can control the chaos in your life?) I found papers dating back to

college days, because I save everything (not *everything*, not Mel).
I came across a yellowed loose-leaf page that had his writing on
it. And I saw us in that Chinese restaurant on one of our first
dates. I was a college student majoring in Creative Writing, he
had a degree in English Literature. He wrote better poetry than
I did, so I'd bring my poems to him for criticism. Right there
in the restaurant, he had pulled out a pencil and written on this
paper: "I'll read your stuff if you stop using the following words
so much." Followed by a long column in his half-illegible scrawl:
"time, eternity, love, death . . ."

I carried the fragile paper into the bedroom where he was
resting, worn out from the latest bout of chemotherapy.

"Remember this?" I asked.

Glancing at it, he managed a faint smile. "You married me
anyway?"

I married him anyway. Married him "until death do us part,"
the words we blithely utter when we're so young we're sure that
death belongs to some far-off country we'll never have to visit.

"APRIL IS the cruelest month . . ." That was one of his favorite
poems. And April was when we started on the medical merry-
go-round. (Why does every widow have horror stories about
doctors?)

Ours began with the liver specialist Mel had been referred
to, Dr. X, an obese German.

"Doesn't look good, does it?" That's how he greeted us. Mel's
CAT scans were dangling on the wall from clothespins, like
laundry hung up to dry. There were, Dr. X pointed with a
long ruler, two "things" on the liver. "There," he pointed, and
"there." We sat huddled behind the desk, staring at the shadowy
pictures.

The doctor took Mel into another room to examine him. I
walked over to the window and peered through the slats of the
blind at the flowers beginning to bloom. What a hopeful time
spring is.

When they came back, Mel look relieved. But Dr. X was puzzled because he hadn't found any indication of colon cancer, which he said is usually the cause of liver tumors. He seemed disappointed. "Maybe cysts." He shrugged. "Maybe benign." But he scheduled a biopsy.

We drove home jabbering hysterically, "Benign! Of course!"

That's when the first of my insanities began. I had secretly been bargaining with God: Don't let it be serious, anything else—not the children!—but didn't that leave *me*? So if Mel didn't have cancer, *I* would—because disaster had staked us out, one or the other. My introduction to the way guilt weaves through this: did I really want to be the one to die?

After the biopsy, we were told to call Dr. X for the results. Mel asked me to phone. "You'll be gentler telling me," he said.

It dragged on for days. The results weren't in. The doctor was away. The doctor was "busy."

Finally, an ominous message from his nurse. "We've gotten the results. The doctor wants to talk to you himself."

"Now?" My hand was so damp I had trouble holding the phone.

"He's seeing patients. He'll get back to you."

Two hours later I called again. "He hasn't forgotten me, has he?" I asked the receptionist.

"You'll have to be patient," she said. "The doctor has a very busy schedule."

Unable to work, I sat staring at the phone. By noon it had rung three times, always Mel. "No word yet," I lied.

By 3:00 I was ready to drive to Dr. X's office, storm past those other patients.

At 4:30 he called.

"Not absolutely certain . . . but a good chance they're malignant."

A "good" chance? What would a bad one be?

Dr. X was scheduling Mel for a colonoscopy at the local hospital. Those words shook me out of the paralysis I'd been in for days. I didn't want Mel at that hospital. It had to be the best.

Two people we knew had been successfully treated for cancer at NYU Medical Center in Manhattan; surely that meant *something*? I called my friend Dorothy, whose husband had had a successful cancer operation there and asked for the name of their doctor.

Then I called Dr. X's receptionist and told her I was coming over to pick up the CAT scans.

"You'll have to speak to the doctor about that," she said. No delay this time, he'd be on the phone in a minute.

"Just have them waiting at the desk." I hung up before he could come to the phone.

When I arrived, the receptionist reluctantly handed over the manila envelope. "The doctor wants to speak to you."

He came out of his office immediately.

"It's not because of you," I told him. "It's the hospital. I want my husband at NYU."

He walked toward me, eyes dark with fury. I took a step backward, clutching the envelope. He followed me through the reception room, out the door, onto the stoop.

"What you think," he shouted, "you get a miracle?"

"No, no . . ."

"The guy will be dead inside four years!"

I ran down the steps. Forgetting to turn off the alarm, I opened the car door. The siren screamed into the air as I stood there staring into the gray sky, trying the words out aloud.

"My husband probably has cancer."

And all the time I was trying not to hear those other words, words I was going to have to hide from Mel:

"Four years."

Oh, Dr. X, trying so hard to hit at me, you weren't even on the mark.

Mel had twenty-three months left.

3

THE FIRST DAYS. People keep coming into the apartment, carrying boxes of cakes and cookies. To sweeten the taste of death? Neighbors arrive with endless casseroles. "That looks delicious," I say, surrounded by mountains of food I can't eat. What do you do with eleven chicken casseroles?

People seem surprised at how I'm acting. "You're so *up*," someone says. I feel as if there's something wrong with me. But I can't cry. The hostess in me smiles politely, chats about trivial things.

Every time the door opens, I look up to see if it's Mel.

My brother-in-law has invited his entire therapy group. Eight men in dark jackets solemnly parade into the living room and encircle Herb. "So what are you *really* feeling?" I hear them ask him.

A man Mel used to work for pays an obligatory call. His daughter comes with him. She's an actress. "I used to be one, too, years ago," I tell her. "Mel and I worked in theatre together."

"Oh, you *must* go back to it," she says in the throaty theatrical voice that brings up the past. "Off-Broadway needs actresses your age. I mean . . ." She blushes.

"Quite all right," I tell her. "I used to play character roles. In those days, I had to draw lines on my face." We laugh together.

Going upstairs to the bedroom, I look at the drawing of Mel's face that an artist drew years ago. It hangs over our bed. "Honey," I say, "you're missing a good party."

I guess I'm a little insane.

The people closest to me start vanishing, like "Ten Little Indians." Our daughter, Tamar, worn out from the vigil at the hospice, goes back to her home in Massachusetts. I hug her good-bye, frightened of the long drive, suddenly aware how fragile life is. Tonight she looks like a vulnerable little girl, not a woman of thirty-three.

"Take care of yourself," I beg her.

Our son David, who's twenty-eight, stays a few days longer. Then I drive him to the airport so he can fly back to Florida where he works as a journalist. Long after his plane has taxied out of sight I stand in the terminal, my face pressed against the plate-glass window.

My sister's been staying with me all week so I wouldn't be alone. But she has to get back to her own life. She says she misses her husband.

On the final evening, Herb stays with me to greet the last few visitors. When they leave, he stands up to go, looking relieved. "Well, that's that," he says. Putting a period at the end of his brother's dying.

I double-lock the door behind him, turn on every light in the apartment, listening to the silence. I have never lived by myself.

"It's just you and me now, baby," Mel used to say after the children had grown up and moved out.

Now it's just me, baby.

I go upstairs to our bedroom. *Our?* That's a pronoun I better get used to not pronouncing. I turn on the radio, loud. Someone's singing a love song. I turn it off.

I'm standing next to Mel's bureau. It's bare on top. What happened to all those medicines and syringes and rolls of gauze? "Get them out of here!" I'd screamed when I came back into the apartment Afterwards. Somebody must have thrown them away.

This is where I stood that other time, too, when I came back from Dr. X, looking at the darkness on the other side of the window . . .

How DO you tell your husband he has cancer? You keep watch through the window until you see him. He has to walk along the path leading into the court, turn, walk a few steps to the front door. That means you have about three minutes from the moment he comes into sight until you hear his key in the lock. You pray for the right words. You hear the downstairs door open and close, hear him call out his usual, "I'm home." He always hangs up his coat in the downstairs closet; that would give you another minute. But this time he comes right upstairs and stands in the bedroom doorway looking at you.

"It isn't benign?" he asks.

"They're not sure," you have to tell him.

"I knew it, when you weren't downstairs. If it had been good news, you'd have been at the door." He puts his hand over his face, ashamed to let you see the tears. "You'll have to be the strong one," he says.

I FALL into bed, praying for unconsciousness. His bed is next to mine, twin beds pushed together to make a king-sized one. He never went to sleep without kissing me.

The room's too dark, even with the lamp on. I go into David's room, unplug his lamp, carry it into our bedroom. Now there's too much light. I can't sleep. I hear something downstairs. Did I lock the door? I go down, check the lock, rattling the knob.

In the half-light from outside, the living room looks like a funeral parlor; skeletal outlines of huge arrangements of dying flowers, baskets of fruit still wrapped in cellophane. I can't bear the sight of those damn fruit baskets. Clawing at the cellophane, I rip off gift cards without reading them; shove apples and oranges and oversized grapefruit into the refrigerator where they'll rot because I can barely manage to get down any food. Just ice cream to soothe the hollowness. Wine to dull the edges. I make a wide circle around the empty chair at the dining table.

"How can you not know how necessary you are?" he was asking as he sat there, trying to apologize because he'd exploded at me for trying to get him to eat.

"But what good do I do?" I said bitterly (because, of course, I couldn't save him).

"You're *here*," he said, groping for my hand. And he started sobbing, this reserved man who had always had trouble revealing his feelings. What strange gifts we get.

I'M FACING the first weekend. I can't be here alone. A friend is giving a dinner party. It seems obscene to go to one, but I can't stay here by myself.

My friend Dorothy, and her husband, Charlie—who survived *his* cancer—are going. "Come with us," she says on the phone. "You can stay overnight at our house, so you won't have to drive home alone."

I feel like Orphan Annie. I do and don't want to be taken care of, do and don't want to be with people. At the last minute I throw some things into my overnight bag, the same one I had with me at the hospice. There's a folded piece of Kleenex in it. I throw it away. Days later, I realize what was inside that Kleenex. A lock of Mel's hair, that I cut from his head. For days I keep searching for it, ransacking wastebaskets that have long been emptied.

People look uncomfortable when I walk into the dinner party. It would be easier if it were Mel, I guess. Aren't men desirable extras to display at dinners? Not like me, sitting here like a raven in my black dress. Someone tells a joke, everybody roars with laughter. "Mel would have liked that one," I say. The laughter stops abruptly. Am I not supposed to mention him?

The attractive woman I'm sitting next to is holding her husband's hand. Under cover of the laughter, she confides that he's her third husband. She'd been widowed twice; each time she remarried within months. "I was determined to be happy," she whispers triumphantly.

"Keep busy," everyone advises me. "It will help."

How the hell do *they* know?

No ONE warns you that home becomes like an unfamiliar hotel room. There's a woman I hardly know, who goes there to shower and try to sleep, in-between all the running away.

She opens a kitchen cabinet. There are dishes she doesn't recognize. Oh, yes, they're the ones bought for the dinner party they never gave. She had wanted a set for ten, to be sure to have extras; he had said that was "extravagant," eight was enough. The absurd things couples argue about. You worry about breakage, then *he's* the one that's gone.

Why are the newspapers from weeks ago piled on the chairs? What are all those unopened magazines with the mailing jackets still on them? The bonsai she gave him is dying; she must have forgotten to water it. He'd be upset about that; he had fretted over it as though it were a baby. *All* the plants are dying; doesn't the woman who lives here care?

The dining table is heaped with mail, unopened. Condolence cards. Bills. Envelopes from the Radiology Department. Visiting Nurse Service. Hospice. There's a renewal card from a magazine he used to subscribe to. LAST CHANCE it says.

Someday the woman who lives here or at least pays rent here (did she remember?) is going to have to answer all that mail. At least he doesn't have to read all those cards, pay all those bills.

For the first time in thirty-nine years, they have different addresses. His is:

Riverside Cemetery
Plot 12, Row E

The phone rings, shrill in the silence. She makes no move toward it. The ringing goes on and on. Someone doesn't want to give up.

"Hi, baby," he used to say when he'd call at five-thirty. "I'm just leaving the office. Anything you want me to bring home?"

"Just yourself," she would say. Or did she? Maybe she asked him to pick up some groceries.

The phone stops ringing. Someone has given up.

Late one evening when the phone rings, she grabs it, needing *someone*.

"Have you selected a monument yet?" a voice asks.

Nights, she prowls through the rooms, unable to sleep. She finds herself standing in the bathroom, looking into the medicine cabinet. His things are still there. His razor. A small pack of blades. Holding out her arm, she places a gleaming silver blade flat on her wrist, across that pale blue line. But that's not how you do it, is it? You have to find the artery, find your pulse. She'd never been good at finding the place where you feel your blood beating through. But some part of her is watching herself watching the blade, and saying, don't be stupid, unfair to the children, you're supposed to be a grown-up.

She puts the blades back into the cabinet. It helps to know they're there.

"Do you want me to go with you?" she had asked those last weeks.

"You can't," he said.

Chances are, they'll never see each other again.

"I'll be as close as God permits," he promised. How close does God permit?

"Are you here?" she asks over and over again, standing alone in the bedroom.

On her bureau there's an envelope that was handed to her by a neighbor who'd been widowed years ago. In the middle of the night she opens the envelope. The woman has scribbled, *"Survival is worth the effort."*

"SURVIVAL?" I ask, staring at myself in the mirror. My hair is grayer overnight, my eyes are empty.

Maybe I should begin by opening those condolence cards. "I will miss him," everyone writes. (*You* will miss him?) "The world is poorer" . . . "never see his like again" . . . "what a fine man . . ." Are there stock phrases people can find somewhere? If he was so "fine" (and God knows he was), what kind of fool was I to have ever fought with him?

I shove that mountain of cards into shopping bags. I'll answer every single one of them. "Nobody answers all of them," somebody told me. I don't care; *I* will. I'm still taking care of him, aren't I?

There's one envelope I hesitate over. It's from Mel's oncologist. Opening it, I read the brief note, hug it against me. That kind doctor has written that he thinks Mel's finally being able to come to terms with his dying was due to the "wonderful support" his family gave him.

But I'm back in that other afternoon, hearing the doctor say, "You will be the Care Partner . . ."

4

WE HAD THOUGHT cancer was cancer. But we learned that the doctors had to determine the original site, so they'd know how to treat him. The beginning of an education we'd never asked for.

"If you know anything upsetting, don't tell me," Mel kept saying.

"I don't know anything more than you do" (*"four years, four years, four . . ."* drumming through my head).

Still, we clung to the fragile hope that it might not be cancer after all. Wasn't the biopsy inconclusive?

Our first stop was Dr. C, the abdominal specialist who had treated Charlie. A rarity, Dr. C seemed concerned about the patient's fears, not just his blood count.

"I'm scared shitless," my eloquent husband told him.

"Let's see what's doing before you get upset."

"We have a trip to Italy scheduled," Mel said, encouraged. "Okay to go? It's just two weeks." (Traveling suddenly seemed less frightening to him!)

"I really can't recommend that," said Dr. C, looking away. Instead, he scheduled a colonoscopy.

The night before, Mel was more upset about the quart of laxative he had to drink than about the test.

"It tastes awful," he said, glaring at me as if it were my fault. He took a few more gingerly sips. "Nothing's happening."

"You hardly drank any."

He sat watching the clock. Suddenly, with a shout, he raced upstairs.

Half an hour later he emerged from the bathroom, looking green.

"I'm not drinking any more of that stuff! And don't tie up the bathroom, I may need it . . . *fast*."

I laughed.

"What's so damn funny?"

"I'm sorry, but you look so indignant."

He grinned sheepishly. "I guess I am."

We clutched each other, screeching with hysterical laughter.

Nothing showed up in the colonoscopy. Nothing in a stomach examination. Maybe the tumors were benign!

But Dr. C had something else in mind. The hospital was conducting an experiment, a form of nuclear testing that could show far more than CAT scans. Mel was "lucky," he was informed, because he qualified for this free test.

Two days later, we entered the world of nuclear testing. Ironic, because we'd argued so much about nuclear energy. I'm opposed to nuclear plants; Mel thought people like me weren't taking into account the useful things that could be achieved. (Like finding your husband's cancer?)

He was taken into a room that looked frighteningly like an operating room. I was allowed to stay with him. He had to lie still on a table while a large circular dome moved very slowly over every inch of him. A TV-like screen showed the inside of his body in cartoon colors . . . searching, searching . . . a ghastly treasure hunt. When the dome moved over his face he panicked. A lifelong fear of suffocation.

"I'll sing to distract you," I said, barely able to carry a tune.

"That's all right," he muttered, tone-deaf anyway.

They didn't find anything. We began to hope it might be a false alarm. But we were told to return the next day.

Again I sat for hours staring at the lurid colors on the screen. Then around what I guessed was the liver, spots doing a lively dance turned a bright reddish-orange. I heard Dr. L, the physician in charge of the project, whispering to her assistant. Turning, I saw Dr. L nod, her hand going across part of her chest in a gesture that looked like she was getting ready to cut her throat.

There were "two small things" at the entrance to the left lung, she told us later. There was also, she added, "suspicious activity" around the liver. She left us alone to digest the news. Mel sat hunched over, staring at the floor.

"It could be worse," I told him.

"How could it be worse?" he asked hoarsely.

"She said it's treatable, not like something they can't do anything about."

Dr. L was standing in the doorway, all expression erased from her face.

Weeks later, I met her again, while I was waiting for Mel to finish one of those endless tests. I debated about asking her something; the masochist in me won out. "Will they be able to get him into remission?"

She hesitated, then sat down beside me. "No," she said gently, "but they can slow it down."

THEY WERE all so pleased to have found "it." But Dr. C couldn't be Mel's physician because the tumors weren't in the abdomen. He'd have to go to the "chest man." (The medical profession turns your body into a map, each doctor guarding his own territory.)

The chest man turned out to be half our age.

"I'm scared shitless," Mel announced again.

Dr. N ignored him. "It seems there are two small tumors at the entrance to the lung."

"Does that mean lung cancer?" Mel forced himself to ask.

"Not necessarily. I have a hunch they originated somewhere else."

"How could I have lung cancer?" Mel went on, as though arguing with God. "I don't smoke."

Dr. N shrugged. "It's like Russian roulette."

"If it does turn out to be lung cancer," Mel asked, "is that one of the better kinds to have?"

"No," said Dr. N, "that's not the kind you want to have." He sounded like a car salesman.

"But the biopsy isn't definite," I said.

"I'll have *my* man look at it," he said, obviously contemptuous of anyone else's "man."

We went home clutching at the last remnant of hope.

Late Friday night, Dr. N phoned. "Positive! No doubt about it." He sounded triumphant.

Couldn't you have waited until Monday, I thought, and let us have our weekend? No way to hide this from Mel, he'd heard the phone ring. I didn't want to lie to him, it would undercut his trust in me. "Evasion" is the civilized way.

"He'll need an oncologist," Dr. N was saying. "I'll call Dr. G. He's the best in our group."

Apparently they were going to treat him for cancer of "uncertain origin." (They never did determine where it originated, although the final theory was that it had started in the gall bladder and then, having metastasized, disappeared.)

Days passed. No one contacted us. Even Dr. N was "unavailable." I panicked. Time was vital, wasn't that what Dr. C had indicated when he vetoed our trip to Italy? I called him for help. He also had a "best" to recommend, but this one was Dr. S. "I'll give him a call."

We waited another three days. Four. Meanwhile, Mel went to work each day. (He was the editor-in-chief of Successful

Meetings, a top trade magazine in the travel field.) The job was a "godsend," he said, because it was distracting.

I wasn't as lucky. A free-lance writer, I work at home alone. I'd sit at the computer, trying to concentrate. My "distraction" was thinking about our lost trip. If no one was in that much of a hurry, why couldn't we have gone to Italy, ridden together in a Venetian gondola like luckier—healthier—lovers? Besides, I'd think, staring at the blank screen, would the treatments really make any difference? Wouldn't it be better to try to enjoy whatever time was left? Or would that destroy any chance they might save him? Better, not better, like picking off petals on the daisy.

Another day passed. A week. Had everyone forgotten us? I called the oncology office, pleaded with the secretary to put me through to Dr. S, Dr. G, *anyone*. But they were all, it seemed, as unreachable as royalty. In a moment of inspiration, I remembered Dr. L's saying she was so grateful for Mel's "cooperation" with the nuclear project, she'd be glad to help in any way. I called; she was out of town. I debated taking Mel to another hospital, but that would mean starting over. Time, time, running out . . .

The phone finally rang. Dr. L's assistant, wanting to know what the problem was. Shamelessly sobbing into the receiver, I told him. He said that by a "lucky coincidence" Dr. S owed him a favor. See what he could do. Get back to me right away.

Another day passed. Another. The assistant called back. "Unfortunately," Dr. S was leaving for a vacation.

"Wait!" he broke into my hysterical explosion, that elusive doctor had been willing to assign Mel to an oncologist in the group: a Dr. Hohlman. "Call for an appointment."

Same initial as ours, I thought, looking for good omens.

So Mel finally got an oncologist. But no one had bothered to inform Dr. Hohlman that Mel was to be his new patient. The CAT scans and nuclear results were in some other part of the hospital, but no one seemed to know where! Dr. Hohlman's first act when we were ushered in was to throw up his hands in exasperation. (For the next year and a half, I kept seeing him throw up his hands in that same gesture, perennially frustrated by some bureaucratic "stupidity.")

"Qué pasa?" he asked Mel. He's not Spanish, just a nice American Jewish doctor, but *"qué pasa"* was the greeting he always seemed most comfortable with.

". . . scared shitless . . . ," Mel gave his usual refrain.

"We'll give it our best football try," Dr. Hohlman said.

"That wasn't very reassuring," Mel muttered, when the doctor left the office for a moment. "He could have told me I'd be fine."

"I'm sure that's what he meant," I said, crossing the line into lying.

But Dr. Hohlman followed up his football forecast with something more to the point: Mel would start chemotherapy immediately with a monthly five-day stay in the Co-op Care unit of the hospital. And I would stay there with him as his live-in "Care Partner."

"Great," we said. (The two of us, who used to be guests at five-star resorts during Mel's trips, so enthused at the "invitation" to share a hospital room!)

Asked if he had any questions, Mel came up with his second biggest fear. "Will I lose my hair?"

Dr. Hohlman ran a hand over his own nearly bald head.

"Yours will grow back."

5

It's not possible he isn't *somewhere* in the world. All these thousands of people walking past on the street and not one of them can ever be him? Not possible that when I open the door he'll never be here, arms out to give me a hug. "I'm back," I call out each time I come home.

"What does death mean," a friend whose father has died asks me, "when I still expect to hear his voice on the phone?"

The therapist I've been seeing for years (who was also Mel's therapist) tells me, "Get on with your life."

"But I can't do anything," I tell him. "Can't eat properly, can't deal with the bills, can't even write. Most of all, can not be in that empty silent tomb of an apartment! Hear me?" (I'm always angry these days.)

"What *can* you do?" Dr. Ruben asks.

"Keep running."

But no matter how much I run ("You're doing so well," people tell me, relief in their voices), there's always the coming home. The desert days stretching endlessly ahead. It's a major achievement just to get out of bed each morning. I keep taking hot baths because I'm constantly chilled, but I can't seem to get warm. I'm retrogressing into a scared little girl, huddled under the blankets. I wish someone were here to tuck me into bed each night, leave on a night light in case I have nightmares.

I run to my sister, Sonia, in Maryland. It seems purposeful to be getting on a train like a normal person. My sister is caring and supportive; my sister is married. I see her husband come home from work, kiss her, ask how her day was. Sometimes it's lonelier being with people.

I yearn to visit Tamar and David. But rule number one is Thou Shalt Not Lean On The Children.

"How did you tell them about Mel's illness?" people ask.

By telling them the truth—but not the whole truth—not until I had to.

I'm back in that eternal replay when I had to tell Mel that the "things" on his liver might be cancerous. We were still standing there clutching each other when the phone rang. I prayed it was a wrong number or an organization wanting money; anyone to whom I wouldn't have to say "our news is terrible."

It was David. "Any word about the biopsy?"

"They're not sure," I told him, picking my way carefully around the truth, Mel listening.

He and David were so close. They played silent games of chess, noisy games of handball, had a joyous rivalry about their baseball teams (Mel stubbornly loyal to the Giants, David a Cubs fan). When Mel was ill, David called almost every night. "How's Dad doing?" he'd ask me. But when I put Mel on the phone, all I could hear was baseball talk. David's way of saying "I care" was, "Your Giants aren't doing badly." (The Willie Mays shirt he sent Mel must be in the closet I can't make myself open.)

"I'm sure it will be fine," David was telling me. It was the optimism he held on to for nearly two years. I think he couldn't imagine being without his father. On Washington's Birthday weekend, during a remission that did, incredibly, happen after all, we visited David in Jacksonville. The three of us sat in a lively Creole restaurant, surrounded by people laughing and talking. Mel was silent, sunk in depression, never really believing the remission would last. David said, "You two are going to be a lot happier a year from now." It was almost a year to the day of Mel's death.

Our daughter, on the other hand, was pessimistic from Day One. But Tamar had just been through the deaths of two friends. She sent Mel a stream of get-well notes with rows of "XXXX"s kissing him by mail. Often she'd visit us at the hospital, riding all the way from Massachusetts and back in one day, long enough to hold her father's hand and tell him she loved him. Mel, so quick to pick up vibes, would tell me afterwards, "She's afraid I'm dying." But Tamar's pessimism—realism—helped him near the end, when he could talk to her about his fear in a way he didn't with David.

One weekend Tamar came to the apartment to help us. She spent the time fixing the broken wheel on the shopping cart, rewiring the plug on the vacuum cleaner, hanging up a new holder for the ironing board. As if, by repairing these things, she could somehow fix what was unfixable.

I had to be so careful not to inflict my terror and neediness on the children during Mel's illness. But I have to be even more careful now. They have their own grief to contend with, don't need to be burdened with mine. (Isn't that the attitude you're supposed to have? But inside you're screaming, "Don't abandon me.")

"Up and down," I tell them, when they ask how I am. But one lonely Saturday night, David catches me off guard. I weep hysterically into the phone, then spend the rest of the night worrying that I've upset him. In the morning I phone and leave a message: "Sorry . . . bad day . . . better."

Hanging up after talking to a machine, I ask Mel, "Are *you* here?"

It's what I hear myself asking him over and over again.

* * *

THE APARTMENT is too full of him—and too empty of him. One morning I open his closet, look at the suits hanging there, pressed, just as they came back from the cleaners. Waiting for the thin eager body to put them on, hurry downstairs to go to work, kiss me and say, "Talk to you later." I close the closet door.

His bicycle is standing in David's room. Mel and I loved riding together. That day he went for the first CAT scan he came home afterwards, instead of going to the office. So unlike him. Did he sense that the clock had begun to tick? "Let's go for a ride," he said. It was a windy afternoon, and he zoomed on ahead of me as usual, while I tried to keep his familiar gray jacket in sight. But I couldn't shake off a premonition of the street empty, no Mel riding ahead, waiting at corners for "slow-poke."

We rode to a nearby park and sat on the grass. He was silent, his arm around me, looking at the clouds drifting over our heads. "You're going to live to be ninety," he suddenly said. "It's in your genes." What shadows in his mind made him say that?

"Yours too," I said, as though beseeching him, meaning his father who was ninety-two.

After Mel got the diagnosis, he told me not to say anything to his father. "He'll just get upset and that's not going to help."

But one night Mel stood in the kitchen doorway, nervously tapping on the phone. "I'm going to tell him," he said. "I want him to be concerned about me."

"I'm sick," Mel told his father over the phone.

"What's the matter?" Instant apprehension, built in from death-around-the-corner terrors of a Russian childhood.

"I have cancer."

"No!"

"It's all right, Dad, they've caught it early."

"No . . . no . . ."

"Dad, please don't be upset. Please, don't worry."

"Well, well," said my father-in-law, coming up with his invariable refrain, "I'm sure everything will be all right."

"Yes," said Mel, "it will be all right."

I'm surrounded by things I can't bear to look at. Under the bed, there's the sneaker I couldn't get on his foot that morning when they took him to the hospice. I can't move that sneaker; I always vacuum around it.

Those photographs on our bedroom walls. That wedding picture of those two grinning kids. Next to it, there's an obviously posed photo of a much older couple in formal wear. When was that? Oh, yes, during one of Mel's business trips that we went on together. Colorado. We went river-rafting there. I love all water sports, but Mel was afraid of the water. (We used to laugh about our different fears. I'm terrified of flying, his idea of fun was to go in sightseeing helicopters.) Still, he went with me on that rafting. It was tame, geared to tourists, but he didn't like me to say that. "That river was rough," he told our friends afterwards. Why did I laugh at him? What would it have cost to tell him he was brave? There's a color photo of us on that trip next to the other pictures. I look gargantuan in all that inflated life preserver clothing. Mel's behind me, head ducked down in fear. "I look so fat," I wailed. "But *you* don't look scared out of your wits!" he said. I can't look at these pictures, either. And I can't take them down.

In the drawing of Mel's face that hangs over our bed, he looks so young, the way he did before illness turned his face haggard and old. He had posed in his office, and the drawing shows his neatly parted hair, carefully knotted tie, starched shirt collar. His Editor persona. The assured side of him.

He kept going to the office until the very last weeks. Kept going on business trips (armed with the names of local doctors). He never gave in.

"I'm not courageous," he told me when he was ill.

"You are," I said, almost shaking him.

I mean, what the hell is courage on a *raft*? But it's late to tell him that, isn't it?

I'VE FORGOTTEN to pay the rent. I run over to the rental office in the dark to put the check through the mail slot. As I get near the office door, something sticky brushes against me. During the night I wake up itching badly on my right shoulder. I know what brushed against me, I think, the wings of a bat! I must have been bitten by a bat. I'll go crazy if I don't get a rabies shot right away. I should go to the emergency room, but that's the local hospital, the one where Dr. X is, where Mel had the biopsy. I can't go there. I'd rather go mad. In the morning my shoulder's itching even more. As soon as the rental office is open, I phone. "I seem to have been bitten by something near the office door," I tell the secretary. "Has anyone reported a similar incident?"

"I haven't heard anything. You probably disturbed a spider web."

"That's what I think," I tell her, trying to sound rational. "There aren't any bats around, are there?"

"Bats!"

She must think I'm a lunatic; the word will spread, that Widow Lady, she's gone clear off her rocker.

I run away again, this time to a yoga center in the mountains. The grounds are dull brown in March, the trees skeletal. I take yoga classes, meditate, have the first meals I've been able to eat, in a cafeteria where "silent eating" is the rule. I'm grateful not to have to talk to anyone. The guru addresses an audience. "Pain is the gateway to wisdom," he says.

I go for solitary walks in the woods. The yoga leaders have told me pain is less if you're able to "stay in the moment." Trying, I study a miniature waterfall frozen on the side of a rock. For a few minutes, I'm actually able to forget. But I have trouble staying in the moment. The slide show's always running. Hospital. Co-op Care. Hospice.

It's three weeks. Only three weeks? I've never gone this long without seeing him. I stand under a sky blazing with stars. Mel liked looking at them through his binoculars. I'd like to know which is the Little Dipper, where Mars is, but without him to point them out to me I don't even know which are stars.

"Give me a sign," I beg him. The only response is my breath, visible in the icy air. In the light from the building, I can see my shadow moving ahead of me. For a second, I see two! "You *are* here, aren't you?" I call out, mad with joy. But as I take a step, the shadows become one.

My body constantly aches, my shoulders are sore. The Center provides massages. But lying face down on the table, with the masseuse's hands stroking me, I have to fight off tears; even this reminds me of Mel. "I love your body," he used to say, caressing me. I have to pay to be touched now.

When her hands reach my right shoulder, the masseuse says it's so knotted up she doesn't know if she can do anything about it without hurting me too much. Coming around to the front of the table, she asks, "What happened when your husband was dying?"

I'm shocked by the question. "I don't want to talk about it."

"Perhaps you need to."

"It would make me cry. I don't like to cry in front of anyone."

"Perhaps you need to," she says again.

I burst into tears, trying to breathe through a nose that's so clogged I feel as if I'm suffocating. "For a long time," I push out the words, "I was the only one who knew he was going to die."

"That's a lot to carry on your shoulders. No wonder they hurt."

I kick at the table in rage, grab the Kleenex she's pushing toward me. "We stayed in a place called Co-op Care . . ." I can't breathe.

She waits.

". . . lived there with him . . ."

I begin to tell her what it was like. All the things I've never shared . . .

I'VE BEEN crying for a long time. There's silence. I rest my head on my folded arms like a child.

She puts her hand on my shoulder.

"The knot's gone," she says.

6

It was Memorial Day when we first went into Co-op Care. The expressway was bumper to bumper with people going in the opposite direction, leaving the city for a fun weekend.

Co-op Care is a rarity in the American medical scene because it allows the patient to live in a private room in a special section of the hospital, with a personal "Care Partner." ("It's our Howard Johnson set-up," Dr. Hohlman told us.)

Co-op Care also lets the patients retain some feeling of being in control, because they're allowed to be mobile and to go to their doctor's appointments and treatments rather than being confined to bed, helpless. This was important for Mel, who needed to feel he wasn't an invalid. (With incredible denial, he persisted almost to the end in describing the tumors as "on" the liver, not *in* it, so he wouldn't have to admit that it was liver cancer.)

But the Co-op Care unit often seemed like a stage set for a vacation in Hell: spectacular views of the city from a glass-enclosed solarium, weekly films, a "Happy Hour" (non-alco-holic)—and meanwhile we were all dealing with death.

The top seven floors of NYU Medical Center are set aside for these privileged twosomes. Five of the floors house the living quarters: identical rooms, behind large wooden doors. Inside each room there's the same dark brown motel-style furniture: two narrow beds with thin, flat rubber mattresses, a night table for the essential phone, bureau with a small refrigerator on top of it, TV, two ugly leather armchairs under the window flanking a low square formica table. All the comforts of home and every-thing washable, including the carpet, for all the times the patient throws up from chemotherapy. Each room we checked into had a faint aroma of vomit.

The only things that distinguish one room from another are the varied prints (always two) meant to brighten the walls, and the view from the windows. The choice ones face the river. When we were given our room assignment the first time, I asked for a river view. As if this were the Hilton.

"You're lucky he has any room at all," said the admitting clerk. There's a long waiting list, not only for cancer victims, but those with heart disease, and swelling numbers of AIDS patients.

We checked in a total of twelve times, five days each visit. The first thing you have to do is pick up badges of identification: pink for the patients, yellow for the partners. CARE PARTNER, mine read. Proud of that identity, I asked if I could keep my badge as a memento when we checked out. The nurse looked at me disbelievingly. By the end of the third stay, I couldn't wait to turn it in.

If our room had the coveted view, I'd feel as pleased as if we were in a Caribbean resort overlooking a moonlit ocean. "Look," I'd tell Mel, "we can see the river."

"What the hell difference does it make?"

But the view helped save my sanity those long evenings when I sat in the chair by the window, unable to read, afraid the TV might disturb Mel as he slept off the stupefying effects of

chemotherapy. I could look from him to the constantly changing scene on the water, lit up in the dusk. The large sightseeing
boats with tourists crowding along the rails looking toward *us*,
comical tugboats that looked as if they belonged in the books I
used to read to the children Once Upon Another Time. One
day Donald Trump moored his enormous white yacht at the
foot of the hospital. I was helping Mel stagger back and forth
from bed to bathroom; in between I'd glance down through the
windows and watch guests arriving for a gala cocktail party.

But *I* was supposed to be one of those guests. Mel had re-
ceived a press invitation and I'd eagerly volunteered to go in
his place. My black silk cocktail dress looked bizarre, hanging
in the cubicle that passed for a closet.

At the last minute, I was too exhausted to go. And it seemed
too macabre to go downstairs to step aboard that fairy-tale
yacht. How could I have chatted with anyone from a normal
world? Eaten from the lavish buffet without thinking of the
nauseated pale people in the cafeteria above? Too bad, I
thought, watching helicopters landing guests alongside the
yacht, I might have met Ivana in her dazzling Dior or whatever.
This was before the headlines broke and the public pounced
on tidbits of a marriage that was rotting.

Ours wasn't. We'd been brought closer, almost welded together. "We" saw the doctor today, I'd tell the children, "we"
got a good report.

The routine in Co-op Care is always the same. Each morning
a schedule is taped to the outside of your door, informing you
of your activities for the day. Swimming at nine, tennis at ten
. . . No, that was in our other life. Doctor at such and such time,
"chemo" (as it's familiarly dubbed, like a pet project) at X hour,
maybe a CAT scan or X-rays—unless you're paged to go to
them at the last minute, at some inconvenient time like when
you're trying to eat. Each visit there's an appointment with the
nutritionist, who advises which foods provide the most nutri-
ents; or would if the patient could get down any food at all,

much less *keep* it down. You can also request a session with the Relaxation Therapist.

"Relaxation." That's the key word on the in-house TV channel. A solemn young man and woman can be seen sitting cross-legged, softly intoning, "Close your eyes, focus your mind . . ." accompanied by soothing music and montages of oceans or meadows that seem light-years away. Mel tried to follow the routines, but quickly gave up. "You don't relax enough to relax," I told him.

A weekly movie is shown on a screen set up in the cafeteria. On Halloween the announcement on the board promised a "ghoulish" film set in a *cemetery*. The man in charge couldn't understand why no one showed up for that movie!

Each morning we had to go to the busy fourteenth floor, where the doctors and treatments are. We'd sit in the line of chairs, waiting for Mel's name to be called. He'd keep knotting and unknotting his fingers, irritated because he had to wait. It wasn't that he had anywhere else to go, but Mel was never one to tolerate waiting, especially in restaurants. (How much of him I seem to have internalized. These days I get incensed if I'm kept waiting. Doesn't everyone realize I'm bereaved, why should I also have to stand on lines?)

He'd have his temperature taken, be weighed, have blood drawn—gripping my hand too tightly because he couldn't get over his dread of needles. "*Qué pasa*, Mr. Hosansky?" Dr. Hohlman would ask each day, probing Mel's abdomen. (Always "Mr.," according him that dignity amid all those indignities.) Even if Dr. Hohlman was reassuring, Mel's radar would pick up something to worry about. "He didn't say . . . He didn't mean . . ." I'd assure him, like a recording.

Then unless "we" were scheduled for tests, we'd be free until the afternoon's chemo treatment.

Mel still liked to read the morning paper, so I'd take the elevator down, walk across the courtyard to the lobby of the main part of the hospital—greedily gulping fresh air and the sight of normal human beings. I'd buy the *Times*, reluctantly retrace my steps, wanting to run away somewhere—any-where—go back upstairs to sit with Mel. Prisoners, both of us. No time off for good behavior.

Sometimes I could talk him into going to the top floor solarium. Sitting there, I counted the boats on the river. He knotted and unknotted his fingers.

Next to the solarium is the cafeteria. Most of the time I'd have to eat there alone because Mel refused to go in after he'd had to dash out to throw up. (It got to the point where he'd feel nauseated as the cab pulled up in front of the hospital.) I'd sit in that cafeteria, hating those other people—the maimed, the wounded, the dying—because they were such constant reminders.

Care Partners joke about the food. It's the only place I've eaten where the chefs don't know how to boil an egg. "Medium-boiled," I'd request each morning. Whoever was behind the counter would glare at me, always surly. (Listen, I'd feel like saying, *I* don't want to be here either.) But the eggs would invariably be either like mucus or rubbery-hard. The last time I went in for breakfast, the man behind the counter snapped, "No medium."

"Okay," I said, since it didn't seem to make any difference, "soft then."

That was the morning they came medium!

Despite everything tasting like cardboard, I gained ten pounds that first year, eating double helpings to fill the insatiable hollowness within.

Patients can get room service, but most of them can't stand to even look at hospital food. A local Chinese restaurant takes advantage of this, with take-out menus slipped under the doors. I tried ordering Mel's favorite duck dishes, or roast beef sandwiches from a nearby deli. He'd just pantomime eating. I was desperate to get food into him; he couldn't afford to lose an ounce. "Get him to eat," Dr. Hohlman ordered, but no one told me how.

Sometimes Mel would have a fleeting craving for a Häagen-

Dazs milk shake. I'd run out to a place a few blocks away, praying they wouldn't be out of strawberry—his favorite flavor—race back before he might change his mind. Once he had a longing for a kosher hot dog on a roll. "They remind me of my childhood," he said. I took a taxi to a deli a mile away to get him one. By the time I got back, he had lost all desire for it.

Afternoons meant chemotherapy treatments. Patients sit in a row, hooked to poles holding plastic bags filled with the potent (and toxic) combination of drugs that may or may not help. Lined up, the patients reminded me of women under the dryers in a beauty parlor. I would sit there with Mel. Sedated, he'd doze, escaping.

I would watch the other people. There was a woman with a French accent whose Care Partner was her teen-aged daughter. The mother always had a dreamy half smile, head held high, moving elegantly through that hall of horrors. The daughter looked morose, angry. They never noticed me.

An elderly couple was having a bout of togetherness cancer. A caretaker stayed with the two of them. (Some rooms are suites, set up for such purposes, even for whole families.) The husband was quiet and withdrawn; his wife the aggressive one, pushing ahead of everyone. Once she made an increasingly irritated Mel wait while she kept making demands of the admitting clerk. "I *insist*. . . We *must* have . . ." A queen in exile.

You could tell which ones were the AIDS patients. They were usually the youngest, in wheelchairs pushed by other gaunt young men. One had his mother with him. I couldn't look at her anguished face.

I was afraid of going crazy, cooped up there day and night. Partners were told we had to be "available" unless someone else took over. But I had no one to fill in for me. I started slipping out for brief walks, like a truant schoolgirl. Later I discovered that none of the Care Partners stayed around the clock. I'd meet them in the elevators. Sometimes we'd ask, "And how is yours doing?" More often we'd avert our eyes, needing a respite from "it." I tried, "Lovely day, isn't it?" "You mean *outside*?"

the partner answered bitterly. One woman came back defiantly flaunting a Bloomingdale's shopping bag.

At night, when Mel was sleeping, I'd escape for a quick walk down deserted streets, less afraid of being mugged than of cracking up. Sometimes I'd go to the busy intersection where there are restaurants and movie theatres—the ones we used to go to on Saturday nights. I'd walk past our favorite Italian restaurant. Through the large plate-glass window I could see people at "our" table, the one in the corner, laughing, chatting, toasting their future. Walking past a movie theatre, I'd get a whiff of the popcorn smell of normalcy, see people casually waiting on line as though life was going on as usual. I'd go to the all-night grocery stores that had buckets of flowers displayed on the sidewalk and buy irises—Mel's favorite flower—to brighten our colorless room, to brighten his face. But everywhere, *everywhere*, couples strolling hand in hand . . .

We had very few visitors, but Mel's younger brother, Herb, came each month. He'd sit there uneasily, trying to make small talk with a brother he'd never been close to, a brother now unable to respond very much; too ill, too late.

A few times Herb or Tamar stayed with Mel on Monday nights, so I could get to my writing workshop, which was only five minutes away by cab. Anxiety-ridden because neither of them could stay the whole time, I'd leave the number next to the phone as if for a baby-sitter. "Back by ten," I'd assure Mel.

"Have a good group," he'd say, wanting me to "enjoy," not to be so tied to him. "It isn't healthy for you to be with me all the time," he'd say. But as I'd start to leave, he'd call out anxiously, "Ten? That's when you'll be back?"

"Say ten-thirty," I'd answer carefully, knowing how fearful he'd get if I was late, "depending on how long it takes to get a cab."

I'd hurry back, breathless and nervous. Usually he was asleep, so I'd feel relieved. And lonely. He wasn't asking his usual, "Did they like your story? How did it go?" The beginning of having no one to tell.

Two Samaritans came every time we were there: Lee and Stan, our closest friends. Knowing what I was going through trying to get Mel to eat, they'd come bearing edible gifts, like homemade watermelon jelly. I'd assure them that Mel would eat it when he was "feeling better." Their visits were a reminder of the wonderful evenings we'd spent together. But it upset me to be seen like inmates of an asylum: Mel gaunt and unshaven in a stained robe, me chattering frenetically, starved for conversation. One night I played hostess, surprising them with a bottle of Chablis I'd managed to chill in the small refrigerator, nuts and raisins set out on the table in paper cups . . . while Mel tried not to see the food and Lee murmured, "Anne, you don't have to, really."

But I *did* —and so did Mel—have to have some semblance of normality. Even laughter. I'd come back from my walks with small gifts that might make him smile, like a thumb-sized teddy bear holding a string, with the caption "Hang In There."

And we had our private joke: the first afternoon we spent in Co-op Care we made passionate—frantic?—love on that impossible slippery rubber mattress. "This is the therapy you need," I teased. But it never happened again.

WHY DOES it all keep coming back, this eternal slide show? Mel was discharged from Co-op Care, won't *I* ever be?

Late at night, when he was safely asleep, I'd go up to the solarium. Needing to talk to someone, to hear a voice, I'd stand by the pay phone with a handful of change, wondering who I could call at that hour, how much it was safe to say. I'd hesitate to call the children if I felt I might sound too needy. Instead I'd phone my sister or a friend. One night I hesitantly dialed the number of Mel's older brother, Norman, who lives in Ohio. Norm's first wife had died of cancer at the age of thirty-two.

"I'm afraid of bringing up painful memories," I told him.

"Call whenever you need to," he said.

Whomever I spoke to would try to reassure me: "Sounds as

if he's doing well." I'd say, "Yes, I hope so" (*four years, four years, four...*).

I'd look through the solarium windows at the illuminated panorama of the city. But across the courtyard I could also see the other part of the hospital. I knew that one day Mel would be there instead of in Co-op Care and that it would be because the treatments were no longer helping.

I remembered that later, when I did look in the opposite direction; from the windows of a room in that other side, into Co-op Care. By then, Mel was much closer to dying. Staring across the courtyard into the solarium, I could see silhouetted figures. And I actually *envied* those unhappy people—because for them there might still be the miracle that never happened for us.

7

Coming back from the yoga center, I open the door to the silence. It's so *there* it chokes in my throat.

As though on cue, the phone rings. "I bet coming back is hard," my friend Blanche says.

"How did you know?"

But Blanche is offering more than sympathy. Am I aware, she's asking, that Cancer Care provides free bereavement counseling? She knows a widow who saw one of the counselors and thought he was "wonderful." Obediently I scribble the name she gives me, with no intention of using it.

"Call!" she says. Her voice cuts through the fog.

The narrow space used as a waiting room by Cancer Care is furnished with armchairs and a carpet, all in dark blood-red. A mournful-looking woman takes her coat off a chair to make room for me, acknowledging an unspoken bond.

The door to the office opens, and a short man with a round

face comes out to greet me. Taking my hand between his, he tells me he's Joseph, the counselor I've requested. He leads me down the hallway to his cubicle of an office.

"Tell me what's been happening," he says.

Shredding Kleenex all over the floor, I tell him how I still expect "my husband" to come home.

"I'm acting crazy," I tell Joseph.

"In what ways?"

"I talk to him, to his picture." I don't mention how I call out "Hi, Mel," every time I walk into the apartment.

Joseph assures me everything I'm feeling is "normal." And that it won't always be like this. "But I want to warn you it's customary to feel worse a few months from now."

For the first time, I realize that no matter how much I keep running, there's no detour around the pain.

Joseph says that Cancer Care allows him to see me for a year. I feel as if a rescue mission is being sent. But can you see *two* therapists? I don't want to have to choose between them. I sense that Joseph understands the landscape of grief in a way that Dr. Ruben doesn't. But I can't give up Ruben; I'm not up to another parting. Besides, there are all those other issues that don't go away.

Joseph says, "Many people continue to see a therapist in addition to a bereavement counselor." And Ruben tells me to get "all the help you can."

The problem is, their approaches are so different. Ruben keeps telling me the only way I'll move forward is by "letting go" of Mel. But I don't want to let go of Mel. I want to go forward, yes, but holding his hand!

Joseph tells me it isn't a matter of one day holding on and the next—presto!—you've let go; it's a "process." Holding on/ letting go . . . that's the pattern, it seems.

But a few weeks later he tells me I'm starting to let go, whether I want to or not. It began, he says, with "anticipatory grief" all those months when Mel was ill.

I wonder if it's easier if your husband dies suddenly. But it must be terrible to say "see you later" and never do. To have him go off to work and be struck down by a heart attack or get hit by a car, without a chance to say, "Good-bye . . . I love you . . ."

BUT WHO IS "I"?

In the waiting room, a woman confides that she, too, recently lost her husband. A married couple, she says, consists of two halves. But a widow, she tells me tearfully, is only "half a person." It makes me feel that half of myself has been amputated.

I find when I'm introducing myself, it's always with, "My husband has just died." Has this become my identity?

I GET a stunning letter. There's going to be a "Mel Hosansky Award." It will be presented by the International Association of Conference Centers, which Mel helped to found. The letter is followed by a phone call from Yvonne Middleton, who was one of Mel's editors years ago, and who now has her own public relations company. Her firm's handling the conference where the award is to be given out.

"We'd like *you* to present it to the first recipient," she tells me.

The invitation scares me. It means going to a banquet at a luxurious conference center in Virginia, the type of setting I used to go to with Mel for his business trips, and being with all those people who knew him. It also involves flying, without Mel to hold up the plane!

"Don't do it," the widow of a well-known professor advises me. "I turn down every request to represent my husband. Why leave yourself open to that kind of pain?"

I call Yvonne back and tell her, "I don't know if I can handle it" (meaning, without Mel, who am I?).

"Anne," she says, "you lived *with* Mel, you didn't live *through* him!

"Besides," she adds, "I'm betting on you to do a lot of living yet."

A lot of "living"? I realize I haven't been looking forward at all, just backward to what was.

"I'll do it," I tell her, "on one condition. I want to say a few words, not just hand over the award like a robot."

Yvonne's also got a request. She'd like some photographs of Mel and the children and me. It seems she's putting together a video that will be shown at the banquet. It doesn't occur to me that I'll have to see it.

This can't be me, getting on a plane by myself. ("How can you be afraid of flying?" a friend asked. "The worst has already happened.")

When the plane does, to my surprise, land safely, I'm whisked by limousine to a huge complex, spread over hundreds of acres. The suite I've been given is too big for one person. There are two beds, two bureaus, two bathrooms—two of everything except people.

I put on the black cocktail dress that had hung in the closet in Co-op Care, waiting for the party on Trump's yacht that I didn't get to. Staring at myself in the mirror, I'm appalled by how haunted I look. How come I didn't bother to get my hair done? I add more rouge, practice turning my lips upward, debate about mascara. It will streak if I cry.

"Mel," I say, chancing the mascara, "don't let me make a fool of myself tonight."

The awards ceremony isn't to begin until after dessert, but the banquet drags on for hours. Everyone at my table is raving about the food, but I don't seem able to taste anything. I long for wine, but don't dare drink. The man next to me is telling me how important Mel was to the whole industry; the mask that's my face tries to smile. I excuse myself for trip after trip to the Ladies' Room, where I hide to look over my speech. It's inadequate, I can't write well anymore, couldn't even come up with a good ending. Maybe I shouldn't speak, just hand over the award and sit down. The Association head, who's MC for the event, isn't thrilled about my speaking anyway. "Spouses," I well recall, are second-class citizens at these functions.

At ten, the program finally begins. There are half a dozen awards and speeches ahead of me. Everyone who goes up to the podium is having difficulty seeing because of the overly bright spotlights.

Then the lights dim for the video. I'm at the first table, right in front of the screen. This isn't going to be any TV-sized film I can avoid looking at; that screen is six feet high!

Suddenly Mel's face appears on it, larger than life. It's the first time I've seen his smile in months. One of my hands clutches the other. Don't you dare, I warn myself. There's Mel as a child with his two brothers, in identical white sailor suits. Mel and me at our wedding, grinning at the camera. Mel with the children during a vacation, the ever-present binoculars and camera hanging around his neck, the familiar battered sunhat sliding halfway down his face. A close-up of us in a sightseeing boat on a Swiss lake during our last business trip together—was that just last year? The camera zooms in on his face. I look into his eyes. Honey, I tell him, this one will be for you.

The lights go on again. I hear a voice announcing how "lucky" they all are; "Mel's wife is with us tonight." (Wife, not Widow, one more time.) Someone puts out an arm to escort me to the podium. The lights are so blinding I can't see. Calmly I say, "Please turn off those spotlights, I'd like to be able to see every-body." Someone rushes to do it. "Thank you," I say. "Now can you make me look ten years younger and twenty pounds thinner?"

There's a burst of relieved laughter; what did they think, that I'd come up here and *cry*? I wasn't an actress all those years for nothing!

Dropping that stilted speech upside down on the lectern, I tell the audience I want to share my favorite "Mel story." We had just been married, he was a graduate student at the University of North Carolina, and we had a summer job as caretakers of a vacant dorm. One day we found a baby thrush on a windowsill, its wing broken. Apparently it had been abandoned by its mother. Mel carried it into our room, lined a shoebox with tissue paper to make a nest, fed the bird with an eyedropper. Weeks passed and the wing healed. He put the bird back on the windowsill, but it didn't seem to know how to fly away. To protect it, he brought it back into our room.

"The next day," I tell them, "I was out on an errand. As I came back, I heard strange words through the door. Tiptoeing in, I saw your future editor-in-chief hopping around the room, flapping his arms [I pantomime], shouting at the bird, '*This* is how you fly!' "

The room explodes with laughter. I tell them how Mel liked helping everyone learn to "fly"—his staff, his peers, his children, me.

I had planned to end with, "If Mel were here, he'd thank you." Uninspired ending. But I find myself saying words I hadn't planned, "If Mel is watching . . ."

And looking toward the side of the room, I see him—nodding, smiling at me . . .

"*We* thank you," I tell them.

They give us a standing ovation.

When the music starts, I escape so I won't have to watch the couples dancing. I walk back to my suite under a heartbreaking full moon, talking out loud to Mel. "Did you hear . . . ? How did you like . . . ?"

"Are you proud of me?" I ask him.

In the silence, I realize what the evening has done: given me back a sense of myself.

The heady feeling fades fast. I'm crying under the blankets in that huge bed meant for two.

Still, I leave with the first glimmering of hope. Maybe I *can* exist. Separately.

But any step forward feels like a step away from him.

8

THE FIRST HOLIDAY without him. Passover. A family time.

I go to my sister's. But sitting at Sonia's seder, I'm more aware of the one who isn't there than all the people who are. *"What ails ye mountains that ye skip like rams?"* Mel's favorite part of the traditional reading. We always let him be the one to recite that. As my brother-in-law intones the words, I flee from the table in tears.

My sister urges me to stay for the second seder the next night. But I told Mel's brother Herb and his wife Vella that I'd come to theirs.

Funny about families. You think they'll hang together after a loss. But death doesn't necessarily unite you.

Mel and Herb were never close, divided by unspoken resentments from childhood. Vella and I have a kind of edgy truce. There's been mostly silence from them ever since the condolence week, even though they live just a few blocks away. The one time I was supposed to have dinner with them, they cancelled. "Too tired."

46

I don't want to go all the way back to New York to spend Passover with them. But I promised. And he *is* Mel's brother. I remind myself how helpful Herb was when we were at Co-op Care.

After a six-hour trip, I arrive home exhausted and tense. I call to ask what time I should come.

Herb answers the phone. "I want you to know why we haven't seen you," he says. "It's because I'm upset about Mel. Of course," he adds, "I know you're upset, too."

"You may be upset, but my whole life is shattered."

"I guess so."

In the skinless state I'm in, his words send me spinning out of control. "There's no relationship anymore," I tell him, "but I'll come because I promised."

I take the phone off the hook, needing sleep. I'm due there at seven; at six, I put the phone back. It rings almost immediately. Vella's shouting through the receiver. It takes me a minute to understand the words.

"You're not coming here and screwing up my seder."

"I don't know what you're talking about. I'm not coming to fight."

But she isn't listening. She's telling me they're also celebrating their daughter's birthday and I'm not to "screw that up too."

Then we're both exploding into the phone.

"It's terrible that you haven't had me over all this time," I tell her—the anguish of six weeks focused on a single target.

"We were never good enough for you, were we?"

"Listen," I say, hating myself for pleading, "I'm not up to a confrontation. I'm hurting, you know?"

"You better learn to contain your anger!"

It dawns on me what she's really saying. "Are you telling me you don't want me to come?"

"Damn right! Screwing up my seder . . ." She hangs up.

I stand there clutching the receiver, staring at it in disbelief. I can see the windows of a neighbor who had invited me to go with her to her daughter's for the second seder. The lights are out; she's left already.

"Mel," I cry out, "can you believe this?"

After a while, I realize someone's whimpering, "Come back, Mel, please . . . don't let me be alone . . ."

This isn't going to help. I either fall apart or figure out a way to get through this night. I open the cupboard to see what food is there. Just a can of salmon and a box of matzos, because I had cleaned out all non-Passover foods.

I don't feel like eating anyway. I light the candles, say the prayer, sip a glass of wine. If you can get through this, I tell myself, you can get through anything.

The phone rings. I grab it. It must be Vella, she's sorry for blowing up, come over, we want you.

It's Yvonne.

"I'm home in bed with a rotten cold," she says, "but I want to wish you a happy holiday and see how you are."

I sob like a baby.

"I see how you are," she says. "What happened?"

I tell her. She curses elegantly.

"Don't waste any time crying over people like that," she says. "Do you realize how many of us love you?"

She tells me to come into the city, she'll fix some chicken soup for us. I tell her to stay in bed and get better, I'll be okay.

"Isn't there anyone else you can see?" she asks.

It hadn't occurred to me to reach for help. That's something you have to learn.

I call Edie, a friend who lives in the next court. She used to come over to talk to Mel when he was on chemotherapy and reassure him, because she'd had cancer too.

"Come right over," Edie says. "We're not having a seder but I'll fix you some dinner."

I tell her I'm not hungry, but I'll come for tea and sympathy.

When I get there the CD is playing. "Isn't that beautiful?" Edie asks, tears in her eyes. "It's Brahms. There's so much in life to enjoy," says this woman who's had three battles with cancer in the past ten years. "When you can hear music like this, why listen to people who upset you?"

Her husband comes into the room. Chuck's an artist. I tell them about a Matisse exhibit I saw in Washington. I don't say how hard it was to go into a museum without Mel, because Edie doesn't go for self-pity.

"Oh, Matisse!" says Chuck worshipfully. He runs upstairs to get his huge volume of Matisse, so we can look at the beautiful reproductions.

It isn't a seder, has nothing to do with religion. But it's caring and friendship. Maybe *that's* religion, too.

So you learn that old definitions of family and friend are changing. Afraid of losing contact with Mel's other brother, too, I tell Norman, and his wife Gladys, what Herb said.

"Is it too hard for you to see me, too?" I ask, feeling like a leper.

"How soon can you come?" they answer.

I'M GOING to have to start planning for holidays and weekends, not sit around waiting for people to rescue me. Flipping through the calendar, I notice how many three-day weekends there are. Memorial Day is coming up, when everyone else will be going off family-style to beaches and picnics to inaugurate the summer. It was Memorial Day weekend when we first went into Co-op Care; how am I going to get through that one? And the Fourth of July? Labor Day? I leap ahead to Thanksgiving, New Year's Eve . . . the calendar's a goddamn mine field.

I promise myself I'll plot holidays and weekends hour by hour. Minute by minute. Make dates in advance. Fortunately, I'm blessed with a lot of friends.

But this doesn't always work either. Going to Sunday brunch with some old friends, I'm suddenly aware that they're all couples. Two of them are planning a summer vacation to the Canadian Rockies. That's where Mel and I went the summer before he got sick. "What did you think of Banff?" they ask me. But I'm seeing us the first evening there, so tired from the long trip and a three-hour delay in the airport that we didn't feel like sitting in a restaurant. Instead, we bought slices of pizza and chocolate-chip ice-cream cones and ate in a little park, sitting on the grass like happy vagabonds. So rare for Mel to act like that. "Remember?" I long to ask him.

No, it doesn't always help to be with friends. There's an abyss between us. I feel as if I'm exiled in an alien country they know nothing about.

How do you get through not just holidays, but the rest of this gray life?

"A day at a time," says Dr. Ruben.

9

CANCER CARE HAS more help available: a bereavement support group for spouses.

Joseph tells me there's room in one that's been meeting for eight weeks. Apparently that's the customary amount of time, but this one has been granted an extension.

Nervously I walk into a room that has no windows. It feels cut off from the world. I'm the first to arrive. There's a large oval table, with a lot of chairs around it. Boxes of Kleenex set out like place settings. Baskets of nuts and raisins. Coffee and tea on a hot plate in the corner.

People start coming. They nod at me coolly, appraising me. I feel as welcome as a new sibling. But a tall woman, graying hair pulled into a knot, smiles and sits beside me.

"I'm Julie," she says. "How long?"

"Seven weeks," I answer, understanding our new time frame.

"Seven weeks!" says the woman on the other side of Julie. She shakes her head. "You're so *raw*."

Seated around the table, finally, are ten women and two men.

They look as if they're in their fifties and sixties, except for one shockingly young woman. "Debbie's only thirty-two," Julie whispers. "She was married less than a year." I stare at that young face, wondering if it's easier if you don't have all those memories.

The leader, a plump sad-faced woman, sits at the head of the table. "So how is everyone?" she asks.

"Just marvelous," a sarcastic voice calls out. "Pass the Kleenex." There's bitter laughter.

I'm silent, rigid. It would be embarrassing to cry in front of these strangers.

But another newcomer walks in. Asked to introduce herself, she unhesitatingly launches into a monologue that goes on for twenty minutes, sobbing as she describes how her husband died in bed beside her because the hospital had erroneously sent him home.

I can't bear the memories she's bringing up. Then I see that everyone else is crying, too, reaching for Kleenex, nervously grabbing handfuls of raisins. It seems that sharing the pain is what a support group is all about.

But we each come into bereavement with old baggage. I feel jealous and angry (a sibling myself!) that this woman is so free to talk about her grief when I'm politely quiet.

Rage: It's sitting at the table with us.

Grazia, a Dutch woman who has no family in this country, is complaining about how unfeeling her friends are about her loneliness.

"You're angry about it," says a grim-faced woman named Louise.

"No, hurt," Grazia says.

"You damn well are angry," Louise shouts. "We all are."

"I know I am," says an attractive woman across from me, "because I was married before and I bumped into my first husband yesterday. All I could think was, *he's* alive, the bastard!"

Madge, the woman who told me I was still "raw," reports that she went away for the weekend and managed to have a "pretty good time."

"Good for you," I say, encouraged.

"But coming back to the empty apartment was terrible," she says.

I wait for some hopeful words. But everyone's head is nodding; everyone's echoing, "Yes, terrible."

I look toward the leader; she's nodding tearfully, too.

Afterwards, we all go to a Chinese restaurant for dinner. I confide to Louise that I think we should be pointing each other in a more positive direction.

"You're looking for us to tell you what to do," she snaps. "Well, we aren't."

I feel like a naughty child. She's right, that's what I want from them. Someone to hold my hand; point north, east, south, west, say, "This is the way to go."

But another part of me objects that we're both right. How can it be helpful to wallow in mutual misery?

I go home depressed, unable to get those desolate faces out of my mind. Am I condemned to being one of the living dead? I call my friend Judy, who's a therapist.

"You have to be careful about groups," she tells me. "Remember that each person is different. Just because one person reacts in a certain way doesn't mean you will. The problem with a lot of women who are widowed in their middle years is that they've never developed an identity of their own. But," she says, "*you* have."

"IDENTITY?" ISNT that exactly what I'm having trouble with? Dorothy invites me to a dinner party. I'll be the only single woman. Single! Impossible to grasp this.

"Won't I make those couples uncomfortable?" I ask her.

"Only if *you* feel that way," she says. "Aren't you an entity in yourself?"

I guess not.

* * *

WE TALK a lot in the group about socializing.

"You can't socialize with couples," says Tess, a red-haired woman whose lips twist bitterly. "They don't want you."

"That's not my experience," I start to say.

"You'll see," she says.

She tells us about going to a restaurant with a couple. As they got to the door, she stood there waiting for the man to open it for her. "A gentleman should do that for a lady," says Tess. "I don't go for this liberation stuff."

But the wife stalked past her and flung the door open.

"Welcome to the real world," she told Tess.

At another meeting, we get into a heated discussion about whether or not to pay our own way. (The women are the ones who bring this up; the men shrug it off as "no problem.")

"I don't expect to have checks picked up for me just because I'm a woman," I tell them.

They all agree. "I make it clear that I expect to pay my own way," says Madge, "just as Jack would have picked up the check for us."

We're all pleased with our show of independence.

But we face a much touchier problem. A widow, it seems, becomes an instant threat to a wife. One friend who'd never displayed any observable affection for her husband before sits in front of me ostentatiously holding his hand. What is this friend of so many years trying to tell me; hands off, he's *mine*? Don't worry, I want to tell her, I still feel married to Mel.

The consensus in the group is that we're better off socializing with each other, "because we're the only ones who know how we feel."

Mrs. and Mrs. Widow, out for a lovely evening.

THERE SEEMS to be some animosity toward Debbie, the thirty-two-year-old.

"You're so young, you'll marry again," Louise tells her bitterly.

"Don't tell me that!" Debbie says. "Listen, I hear all of you crying about being alone after thirty or forty years together. Do you know how lucky you are to have had that? We weren't allowed," she says, her voice breaking, "to have our time."

Later, at our routine Chinese dinner, Debbie tells me she's leaving the group because she needs to branch out from this bereaved scene. It's too "negative" for her.

"I used to be an athlete." she tells me, "and I was taught that how well you perform has a lot to do with your mind-set." She stares at me defiantly, tears in those young eyes. "I'm determined to beat this thing. I don't want to be a loser for the rest of my life."

I CONFESS to Joseph that I have a terrible secret. "I caused Mel's cancer."

"How did you manage to do that?"

"We argued a lot. I got angry about his trips. I didn't accept him the way he was, like he did me. I wasn't tolerant enough when he'd get anxious about being late." I shred more Kleenex. "He hadn't been looking well and I told him he should get a checkup, but I didn't *push* it. If I had, he'd be alive. If I . . ."

"Why do you need to believe that you caused his death?" Joseph asks.

I keep my shameful secret from the group. But one day someone says, "I think it's my fault he died."

"I feel that way about my wife," says one of the men.

The refrain goes around the table. "My fault . . . my fault . . ."

You'd think we were a bunch of murderers.

MADGE INVITES Julie and me to her country house for what she says will be a "relaxing" weekend. But we're no sooner seated in my car than Madge begins an unrelieved travelogue revolving around her husband.

"There's the diner Jack and I ate in the day he got the diagnosis."

"What beautiful scenery," I start to say.

"This is the road we took when Jack had to go back to the hospital."

"It's so good to get away from everything," Julie says innocently.

"We had to stop going when Jack got too sick to drive," the leaden voice goes on.

"It's so good to have you two here," Madge says midway through a very long weekend, "so I can talk about Jack."

But you didn't warn me, I want to say, that this would be a therapy weekend. I know it's healthy for her to "ventilate" her feelings, but I can't ventilate my rage at constantly being pulled into *her* pain. And she seems oblivious to the fact that I'm in the same boat.

I confide my feelings to Julie. She was married to a Japanese sculptor. "I talk about him a lot, too," she says apologetically. "Does that bother you?"

"No," I tell her truthfully. Maybe it's because she resurrects the ways he lived, not just the way he died. She talks about his love for his work, for his daughter, his students. His enthusiasms. His laughter.

Maybe it's also because Julie brings up her husband in a way that feels more like sharing. It's always followed with, "And did Mel . . . ? Did you . . . ?"

I tell Joseph about the weekend.

"It was awful of me to resent Madge. She's so needy. But damnit, so am I!"

Joseph tells me it's important for "widowed people" to learn how to get their needs met. "You could have told her, 'I sympathize with how you're feeling, but it's painful for me to keep listening.' In the future, make a list of what *your* needs are and how you're going to get them met."

I look at him dubiously. "I'm not too good about asking for what I want."

"Honey," he says, "start learning! You've got to take care of yourself now."

10

Widows could use some lessons in self-defense! Not to protect ourselves from muggers, but from the barrage of comments thrown at us by people who may (may not?) mean well.

I tell a friend I'm starting to feel a little better.

"I hear the second year is harder," she says.

I take that remark to Joseph. "If the second year is harder," I tell him, "I'm giving up now."

"It's different for each person," he says.

One rainy evening when the weather matches my mood, I go for a solitary walk—and have the misfortune to meet a neighbor.

"Oh, my dear," she says, "do you miss him much?"

I'm tempted to say, *"Who?"*

She then informs me that despite husbands being "a pain in the neck," she doesn't know how she'd manage without one. I hear that kind of thing a lot lately. ("Who takes care of the car now?" The same one who always did: *me*.)

"Frankly, I'm glad I'm not in your shoes," confides a second neighbor; adding thoughtfully, "How do you manage to sleep all alone there at night? Aren't you worried about prowlers?"

No, just neighbors.

On the other hand, positive remarks can be just as difficult. Every time I hear someone say, "I can't believe how well you're doing," it shoves me right into the Guilt Bag. What right do I have to be doing "well," looking "good," if Mel is dead? Running to the mirror, I'm relieved to see the new gray in my hair, the tight lines around my lips, the dark circles under my eyes.

I'm told that some people "can't deal" with what's happened. Rose, who's one of my oldest friends, likes everyone to be "cheerful." For years we chatted on the phone once a week, but ever since Mel got sick she seems to have misplaced my number.

"I wish you'd call more often," I tell her.

"I would," she says, "but I'm afraid you'll sound depressed."

Then there are those who seem to be checking their watches to make sure you're on schedule for "getting over it." Like the comfortably married relative who's bothered by the fact that I still can't go to movies. "Isn't it time you pulled yourself together?" she asks. I'm in a different time zone, I want to tell her. Instead I say "I'm working on it." That makes *her* feel better.

Some people think they should let you know how well everyone else is doing. One night when I'm dialing every number in my address book just to hear a voice, I call a woman I haven't seen for a while. She says accusingly, "I tried to reach you, but you're never home." I explain—for the twentieth time—how I try to avoid being home, especially at dinner time because that's when Mel used to come home from work. (I can see him walking into the room as I say this. I wave, but he's gone. He never did like to listen in on my phone calls.) Meanwhile, this woman's telling me about meeting "such a cheerful widow," who fills her time by square-dancing. "She goes with groups to all kinds of places. Greece. North Carolina. Fantastic, this lady." Before I can think up a civilized excuse for getting off the phone, she says sternly, "I certainly hope you'll keep *your* chin up."

"Both of them," I promise.

Another [former] friend turned her back on us when Mel was ill. Wanting to mend fences, I decide candor might help. (Isn't honesty supposed to be the therapeutic key to relationships?) So I tell her, "I really needed your supportiveness during those months when he was sick."

"But, hon," she says, "you didn't tell me he was *dying*."

Lilly's husband often works late, so she and I go out to dinner together. (I'm noticing that where it used to be couple-to-couple socializing, the wife gets the job of seeing the widow.) I accept every invitation, trying not to sound as if I'm drowning and she's throwing me a life preserver. (Keep that panic out of your voice if you want a social life, I warn myself.) We usually go to some noisy diner where I listen to Lilly telling me I'm doing "fine," she knew I would. But one night I'm in bad shape. "The truth is," I tell her, "I'm not doing that great . . ."

She interrupts to tell me about someone who's been mugged. "Listen," she says, "you should have *real* problems."

"Mel," I tell the couch when I get home, "I had dinner with Lilly tonight. You're right, she doesn't listen to a word I say.

"Mel," I ask again, "can *you* hear me?"

I'M NOT being fair. Anger's giving me selective hearing. Anger at those women who have their husbands. Women who aren't fair game for gratuitous remarks such as, "I know you'll be strong." (Don't bet on it!)

Some people do know how to tune in to what you're feeling. Our friends Lee and Stan manage to act as if things are almost normal. They keep inviting me for dinner. I think it's hard for them to see me arrive without Mel, but I'm afraid to ask them, afraid I'll be abandoned.

Lee isn't given to emotional displays, so I try to put on that stiff-upper-lip act when I visit them, be "good company." But after I come back from my experience with the masseuse, I warn Lee, "I might cry."

She surprises me by saying, "That's fine."

Why do we think it's "weak" to cry in front of friends?

I'VE DECIDED to wear black for a year. But one evening I'm embarrassed to hear one of the men at a dinner party ask his wife, "You aren't going to look like that when *I* die, are you?"

I hear echoes of Mel, who liked me in "youthful" colors. What am I proving by looking like a bedraggled crow? Are there guidelines for this? (I'm big on rituals these days, they're something to hold on to.)

I call the rabbi for advice.

"Turn toward life," he says.

They're the first good words I've heard.

I buy purple slacks and a bright print blouse, so I'll be in "cheerful" colors when I visit David. (I've decided to brave it and fly to Florida.) But trying on the clothes in the booth, even being in a store for the first time, feels almost obscene. As I leave, clutching my package, I look up at the sky and burst into tears. "Forgive me," I beg Mel.

Planning that trip to Florida, I call the airline to reserve a ticket—only to be thrown by one of those routine questions that doesn't sound routine anymore.

"Is it Miss or Mrs.?" asks the voice on the phone.

"I don't know," I say.

Miss or Mrs. It keeps coming up. I never realized how many times you have to check off those "marital status" boxes. (It's a rare form that includes "Ms.")

I bring it up in the support group.

"I'm certainly not Miss after all these years," declares Madge.

"But we're not really Mrs. anymore," says Julie.

That's one more problem men don't have.

11

I'M MOVING THROUGH the days sideways.

"Go forward," Ruben keeps telling me. But I'm still frantically reaching for Mel's hand. It reminds me of the children when they were learning to walk. They'd toddle a few steps, then turn anxiously to see if we were there.

MADGE SAYS her bereavement counselor told her that by talking to her husband so much, she's not letting his soul "rest." What a guilt trip to lay on us! Am I doing that to Mel? *"Are you here?"* Does my constantly asking him that pull him back reluctantly to this world? I see him beside me wrapped in a pale yellow light. He reaches out his hand, trying to touch my cheek, the way he did in the hospice when he was dying. But he can't feel my skin anymore. I can't feel his fingers.

Maybe he wants to be allowed to rest.

*   *   *

I CAN'T bear to watch couples holding hands. I never noticed before how many people walk two by two. Now all I'm able to see are pairs of hands drifting past me.

I try holding one of my hands in the other to give myself a feeling of being held. My wedding ring rubs against the palm.

The wedding ring. Another issue. We talk about our rings in the group. To wear or not to wear. I notice that one of the women has moved hers to her right hand. "I wanted to see what it would feel like," she says, embarrassed.

Maybe I should try moving mine. Not yet. Maybe at the one-year mark. But that's such an obvious deadline. *Dead*line? That's funny.

I HAVE to get the car transferred to my name. The pen shakes in my hand as I check off the box marked "widow."

"What does widow mean to you?" Joseph asks.

It conjures up an old woman draped in black, heavy veiling from a hat perched like a raven on top of her head, her body shriveling.

When I used to edit newsletters, a "widow" was what I was taught to be careful about, because in publishing it means an extra word dangling at the end of a paragraph, taking up too much space.

"Avoid those widows," the printer told me.

To LIVE alone for the first time, when you're from the generation that went from Parents to Husband, is a 180° turn. There was always someone asking me, "What time will you be home?" Now it doesn't matter when—or if—I come home.

I look at the women I know who are single, as opposed to widowed. They're much younger, in their thirties or forties, a generation that seems to find this solo act easier. One tells me that during her vacation—which she went on by herself—she found a "lovely" restaurant.

"You ate there *alone*?" I ask.

"No," she says, "there were lots of people there."

But I can't go into a restaurant by myself. I prefer solitary dinners on the sofa with "lots of people" on TV.

Weekends loom like large black holes at the end of each week. "What do you do," I ask my single friends, trying not to sound panicky, "about Saturday nights?"

One woman tells me that when she's "between men" she likes to go to the movies. Yes, she says, of course alone.

But I can't walk into movie theatres at all, because Mel loved movies so much. Our Saturday nights. How could I concentrate on a film anyway? If it's tragic, who needs someone else's pain? As for love stories—how could I bear to watch?

"I read somewhere that one is a whole number," Dorothy tells me, trying to be encouraging. But women aren't brought up to believe that one is enough.

Mel's cousin Ruth arrives in New York for a visit. She's divorced, childless, and lives alone in Italy. We meet in a restaurant I used to go to with Mel. ("Are you waiting for your husband?" the waitress asks me.)

Ruth is a tiny woman in her seventies. I don't know her very well, but the few times I've seen her she's intimidated me because she seems so self-assured. "Full of herself," my parents used to say about women like her, as though there were something contemptible about it. Is it better to be *empty* of yourself, the way I am?

"Tell me how you're doing," Ruth says.

"It's hard to be alone," I confess. "I keep running."

"I did that, too, at first."

"When?" I ask in surprise.

"When my husband walked out on me after eighteen years of marriage."

I look away from her, thinking that must be even harder than having a husband die. At least Mel never stopped loving me.

"How did you get to where you are now?" I ask.

"I went to Rome to get as far from memories as I could."

"No, where you are in terms of . . . I mean, you seem so comfortable being alone."

She smiles. "I've learned to enjoy my own company."

"So how do *I* get there?"

She leans back in her chair, thinking about it. "There isn't any formula. At first life was like a totally black night. I'd hear sounds outside my windows—someone whistling, a child crying—and know that somewhere life was going on normally. But I felt utterly disconnected. It was as though I were waiting for someone to wind the spring and get me moving."

"Then how did it happen?"

"At first I did a lot of running and being with people just to avoid being alone. But that gave me a feeling of inner boredom, of heaviness. Finally I asked myself, why was I taking any *scrap* out of a fear of being alone? I was angry about it, and that was a giant step. Then I decided something good might be around the corner if I was willing to explore—and that if it wasn't, I could *make* it happen.

"But it was slow," she says. "For a year, maybe two, I had no desire to cook for myself, no motivation to look nice."

"I know," I say, looking down at the rumpled black slacks and drab sweater I wear most of the time.

"It was three years before I could even go to a movie alone," she says.

"I can't go to movies at all!"

She nods. "But one day I did go, by myself. I thought everyone would notice I was a woman alone. The truth is, nobody cares. Then I got involved in watching the film." She laughs. "When I came out, I felt as if I'd climbed Mount Everest.

"Oh, I admit there are still many times when the sky turns—not exactly black—but a very dark blue, when I feel utterly alone," she says. "But it's important not to brood. Read to the blind, bandage a child's finger . . . but do *something*."

"You're so brave," I tell her.

"It comes from being willing to let yourself experience things. You'll see. Even traveling alone can make you feel a hundred feet tall."

"Someday," I promise her, "I'll make that trip to Italy that Mel and I couldn't have."

FOUR AND a half months. I tell my sister, "Enough already, let's go to a movie."

Her husband comes with us. I see how Jerry's arm rests around the back of her shoulders, the way Mel used to sit with me. I weep throughout the movie, even the comic parts. I don't go to another one.

Watching films on TV isn't much better. One night, restlessly switching from channel to channel, I catch a scene where a man's putting his arms around a woman, pressing his lips against hers in a kiss that seems to last forever. They fall on the bed together.

I click it off. Fast.

12

S<small>EX</small> T<small>HE</small> <small>WORD</small> that's seldom mentioned in the support group.
The only reference is an attempt at a joke by Penny, who's been
widowed the longest.

"I know I should see my gynecologist," she says, "but I'm
afraid he'll find rust."

Uneasy laughter.

Is this part of our lives over? Or are we inhibited about discussing sex in mixed company?

One evening, one of the men is absent. The other has to leave
early. The door no sooner closes behind him than the lid comes
off.

"I want to find a man," says Rhoda, a voluptuous woman in
her early sixties, "but I'm drying up inside. My gynecologist
told me to take hormones." She looks around the table. "You
wouldn't believe the difference! I'm telling you, girls, get a
prescription."

"Masturbation will do it, too," says Louise.

Some heads nod. Not mine.

"I'm not in the mood for masturbation," says Rhoda. "I tell myself I have a headache."

We shout with unfamiliar laughter.

But I go home frightened. I will dry up. Down there. Everywhere.

"Naughty," my generation was told about masturbating.

"Bad girl," my grandmother used to say, slapping my hand.

But a few nights later, lying in bed unable to sleep, I tell myself it might help. "Fantasize," the books advise. I don't want to think about Mel, but I can't conjure up anyone else. It's a long way from Fantasy Land.

My starved body responds. But the unexpected orgasm throws me into a hysterical crying jag, calling out for Mel, caught in the most devastating loneliness I have ever known.

IN THE waiting room before the group begins, Penny confides to me, "I'm nothing without a man."

"But you seem so independent," I tell her, shocked.

"It's an act, honey. Listen, it's been three years. I've got to find someone."

The subject of "relationships" comes up in the group.

"It's easier for men," says Rhoda, looking at the two males accusingly. We all know the statistics, the jokes about lonely widows. What desirable commodities widowers are, balding and all.

But the older of the men, George, who's in his late sixties, is obsessed with his wife. He talks about her constantly, in a reverent tone that keeps her on a pedestal. One evening the group meets in his apartment. It's as if his wife still lives there.

"Everything's just the way she left it," he says proudly, gesturing toward the papers on her desk.

The other man is much younger, in his early fifties.

"I'm looking," he admits, "but I'll never find anything as wonderful as what I had with Sharon."

It turns out that they weren't married. Neither, to my surprise, were Rhoda and the man she speaks of so adoringly. "Ours was a real love story," she keeps telling us. ("That's because he wasn't her husband," Tess whispers.)

But beneath Rhoda's dyed hair and glamorous make-up, there seems something terribly vulnerable. She's the one who moves me the most. Discussing how we told our mates the truth about their illness, Rhoda says, "I told him, 'Honey, we've laughed together and loved together. Now we'll have to cry together.'" Tears glitter on the beaded eyelashes.

Yet she's the one who's now frankest about wanting another man.

Madge speaks for most of us when she says, "I don't want just *anyone*, I want my husband."

I never join in these discussions, cannot even imagine caring about anyone else.

No interest in sex anymore—solo or otherwise.

13

I'M STILL RUNNING. But do I want to run as far as Oregon?

That's where my friend Vanessa lives. She's been inviting me to "recuperate" in her house on the edge of the Pacific. I sit on the bed thinking about going there, holding a large cuddly teddy bear on my lap. Vanessa sent it to me soon after Mel died.

"How did you know what I'd love?" I asked her on the phone, hugging the bear against me.

"I knew."

She sent me a box of chocolates, too. "Here's to a sweet time in Oregon," read the card.

I'm afraid of her.

We used to work together seven years ago, in the editorial department of a large corporation. We both had private offices that weren't very private because the walls were made of glass. This enabled the executives to keep tabs on whether the "goldfish"—as we called ourselves—were really working.

Defiantly, Vanessa hung a large tapestry over her glass wall: two seagulls soaring in the air, against a mustard-yellow sun

70

that's either rising or setting. "For me, it has to be rising," she said (always lecturing me how important it is to keep "evolving").

When she left to go back west, I asked for the tapestry.

"Only if you let those seagulls inspire you to fly," she said. Soon afterwards, I left the security of my job to try my luck at free-lancing. "Evolving," I wrote her.

Vanessa's visited me twice. I sensed that she didn't like Mel. But then she doesn't like men very much. When I met her she was divorced (twice) and had a lover (male). But now she's switched to women.

One of her visits was last year when Mel was ill. She wanted to spend time alone with me.

"I'm seducing your wife away from you for a few hours," she told Mel.

"That's good, because she needs to get away from me for a while," he said. I marveled at his blindness to what sounded like innuendo.

Vanessa and I went to a beautiful sculpture garden and picnicked on the grass. Afterwards, I lay contentedly on my stomach, thinking guiltily how wonderful it was to get away from Mel's sickness, his constant fear, into this sunlit scene. Her hand gently rubbed circles around my back.

"There's something special between us, isn't there?" I asked.

"I've always thought so," she said.

"IT'S BEAUTIFUL here in May," she tells me on the phone.

I hesitate. I don't have the energy for the trip, I'm so tired all the time. And she's too overpowering . . . But a part of me yearns to go.

"Maybe it would be better if I get myself more together first," I tell her. "You don't want me if I'm a weepy mess, do you?" Say yes, tell me I can cry with you.

"No," she says.

Maybe she doesn't want to know how much I love Mel. I used

to air my petty grievances to her, the "he doesn't understand" variety. It feels as if it would be some kind of betrayal to go to her.

"Maybe in the summer," I say, putting the trip on hold—like everything else in my life.

DECISIONS ABOUT money are on hold, too. I can't even open those envelopes that keep arriving from Mel's broker and the bank.

I thought I was such a liberated wife. Free to pursue my own career, a separate bank account for my free-lance earnings. But Mel was the one who paid the bills and decided about investments. I never knew what he was talking about when he spoke of taking out more CDs, adding to IRAs, buying bonds. "You decide," I'd tell him, abdicating.

Now it's hitting me head-on. The will, which should have been a simple process because he left everything to me, has to go to probate. All because of one oversight: those municipal bonds I didn't want to hear about are in his name only. (Everything else is labeled "in trust for spouse.") Probating the will is going to cost about a thousand unnecessary dollars. It's the closest I've felt to rage at Mel since he died.

And there are all those decisions. The broker calls to ask what I want done with the CDs. "They're coming to maturity," he says. (I wish *I* were!) I feel hostile to the broker because his calls send me into a panic. I can't cope with any of this.

Charlie, who's now my lawyer, asks what I want to do with Mel's pension and life insurance.

"I don't know," I mutter, embarrassed.

Trying to deal with all those papers, I shout at Mel, "Why the hell did you leave me with this mess?"

Charlie puts me in the hands of an accountant, who assures me I have enough money to be "comfortable" if I invest cautiously. I don't tell him that I feel threatened, *impoverished*, without the security of Mel's paycheck. The figures are meaningless; truth is, I'd like to hide the money under the mattress.

And I don't tell the accountant—or anyone—about my shameful new habit. That whenever I stop at a takeout place for one of my constant containers of tea I ask for three sugars, even though I use only one. The other two are carried home to be stashed in the kitchen canister. I've yet to buy a box of sugar. I tell myself this saves a lot of money.

We never discuss any of this in the group. (We can talk about sex now, but not about money!) Then Kitty, a reserved woman who seldom speaks, tells us she has a "confession."

"I'm angry," she says, "about the money."

"He didn't leave you any?" we ask.

"Oh, he left me well provided for. But can you believe I'm angry about that? Because now I have to be responsible for those stocks and things." She starts crying. "Every time I walk into the bank, every check I have to sign, just reinforces for me the fact that he's gone."

VANESSA'S SEAGULLS hang in the room where I write. Or try to write. I'm unable to work.

When Mel was on chemotherapy, I tried to keep up with free-lance assignments. Once I brought work to Co-op Care. But it meant interviewing people by phone, and I was too out of the real world there. Besides, the policy at Co-op Care is to interrupt calls whenever the doctors or nurses want to check on a patient. I could hear myself saying, "May I quote you on that?" and a nurse breaking in to ask, "Has he had a bowel movement yet?"

An editor who's been patiently waiting for me to work again asks me to do an article about government agencies. After I've managed to write the first draft, I call her to boast about all the federal agencies I was successful in contacting. There's a gasp on the other end of the wire, but it isn't from approval.

"Didn't you understand the instructions I sent?" she asks. "*Municipal* only."

I run to look at the instructions. There it is—in capital letters—MUNICIPAL AGENCIES.

"Are you all right?" she asks.

"Yes," I assure her, afraid of being crossed off her list of freelancers, afraid I'm losing my mind.

Another editor gives me an assignment. I follow his directions to the letter. But after I've sent in the article, I don't get his usual "great job" call. I phone to ask his reaction.

"Frankly," he says, "it doesn't have your usual bouncy style."

How am I going to be "bouncy" again?

It scares me. I need the work. Not only because of the money, but because I need to feel I'm still a good writer. It's who I am. Not just widow. Not just mother or friend or daughter or sister, all the roles we play. But *writer*. That's who I have to get back to being if I'm to survive.

"You're so lucky you have a passion," Dorothy tells me wistfully. I realize we all need this, bereaved or not.

I try to revise some short stories I wrote before Mel got sick, but it's as if they were written by someone else. So I write about the only things I can focus on: Mel—and survival.

"It's a good idea to keep a journal," I tell the group.

"How does it help?" someone asks.

"You get in touch," I say, thinking about it, "with what you're really feeling, not just what people tell you you're supposed to feel."

But it isn't always easy to look at the truth . . .

14

THE TRUTH? I'VE fallen into a common trap of widowhood. It's called Sanctifying the Spouse. Saint Mel wouldn't recognize himself.

Louise walks into the group and challenges us. "We're all being amnesiacs about our marriages, acting as if they were perfect. Let's try to be more honest."

We look away from her.

I try to remember the ways our marriage wasn't perfect, the ways that Mel wasn't. But guilt—"the crippler," we call it— defeats me every time. "Selfish," I berate myself, cataloguing the ways I failed him.

"*If I had it to do over. . .*" Every widow sings the same refrain. What would we do over? Oh, God, we tell each other, teary-eyed, I'd be more patient and understanding, less judgmental and demanding. A rhyme for the widowed.

If this were a trial separation, what a wonderful relationship we'd have when he came back!

But would we really be so different? When Mel went into

remission those brief months, didn't old grievances surface as though they'd been stored in the closet?

Late at night, I stand on the bed to touch the drawing of his face, run my fingers back and forth over his lips, telling him in Braille that I love him and that I'm sorry for all the ways I failed him.

"Guilt is a way of holding on, too," Joseph tells me.

People tell me I have nothing to berate myself for, that I was with Mel "through it." But they don't know the moments when I was impatient, enraged. Sponge-bathing him day after day toward the end, cleaning out that ugly wound where the tube went into his liver, having to suction that tube—terrified I'd do something wrong that would give him an infection, kill him—and all the time feeling so exhausted, so *imprisoned*, that I—like Mel—wanted it to be over. Finished.

That last week, I told him how I thought I'd failed him all these years. "I contributed, too," he said. "We were too young." Then he said, "For Heaven's sake, honey, no guilt about me afterwards."

Mel, you wouldn't like the way I'm disobeying you.

I come across a prayer that has a startling plea: *"May my memories of the dead be tender and true, not falsified by sentimentality."*

The truth is, I want to tell him, you hurt me, too. Because you were so oblivious to how hard those months were for me. When we had that reprieve and I said, "Thank God, we don't have to go to Co-op Care," you said, "It was hard for *you?*" I wanted to hit you.

But I had to keep my feelings bottled up, because you got upset if I was angry. So I'd explode at the butcher, the woman in the dry-cleaning store, that obnoxious male nurse who came to the apartment to administer the chemotherapy when you were reduced to getting it at home. He hung the bag on a fragile lamp shade. When I protested, he dismissed me with, "Won't hurt it, lady."

I shouted threats at him about a shade that cost, maybe, twenty dollars. You were angry at me about that.

And furious that I kept pushing you to try to eat, to be more responsive, to be hopeful. "I wish you were in my position," you said. A terrible unloving wish.

But how could you *not* resent me for being the one God would allow to go on, like a favorite child? The one who'd live to see what happened with our children, hold a grandchild in my arms, see the roses bloom in our garden again? Once you confessed, "It's hard for me to see David now, because he's young and healthy."

This morning I find a crumpled spiral memo pad in the back of my desk drawer. Opening it, I see almost illegible writing, the only thing I was able to write all those months:

It's midnight and I'm alone in the kitchen mopping his vomit off the cabinet doors.

I see the vomit running down the doors, smell the sickening stench, feel the soggy paper towels leaking into my hands. He hadn't been able to make it up to the bathroom, had staggered to the kitchen sink to throw up, missed it. Now he was upstairs sleeping.

He's dying, does he know it? I die with him, moment by moment. But he's so locked into his own anguish, he has no comprehension of mine. I'm starving for someone to divide this pain with. And my body is so hungry for caresses, for warmth.

"I *need*," I had scrawled, wine spilling on the page, and then, "I H A T E . . ."

YOU'RE AFRAID to think it's God's fault. Easier to think it's yours. So you keep thinking his cancer must have been caused by something you did. Or failed to do. (He looked so thin during our vacation in Canada the year before, why didn't I insist he see a doctor? Whywhywhy?)

During the months of illness, you bargain with God: make him well, please, confound those doctors, refute those statistics, You can do it, God, You can do anything, can't You? I'll be, you promise, so *good*, if only You will spare him . . .

We were given an answer. It was called remission.

In October, during our sixth stay in Co-op Care, Mel had the usual ultrasound. But this time the technician whistled at what he saw. "This is hard to believe."

"What?" Mel asked.

"Looks like the tumors are gone, buddy!"

Mel and I stared at each other, speechless.

We went upstairs for his appointment with Dr. Hohlman. *"Qué pasa?"*

"The tumors are gone," Mel said triumphantly.

Dr. Hohlman beamed like a proud parent. "You've beaten the odds?" But he'd have to see the reports for himself. Meanwhile, go home as scheduled, he'd call us.

I promised God that for the rest of my life I'd never be mean or lie again. And never ever complain. If only, please . . .

The next night, Dr. Hohlman phoned to confirm that no tumors had shown up.

"Does this mean he's going into remission?" I asked, handling the word delicately.

"He's *in* remission."

Mel had to go back to Co-op Care for two more series of treatments as a precaution. On the last day, we stood before Dr. Hohlman as though waiting for a diploma.

"It will be unusual if the tumors don't come back," he said. "But then it's unusual that they went away."

Is it medical ethics to warn don't hope too much?

We went home to try to live like normal people. "Want to take our trip to Italy?" I asked. But Mel was too anxious. Besides, he had to be available for weekly blood tests. I guess neither of us believed it would last.

We talked about getting in the car and escaping somewhere

for a few days—maybe Vermont, where we'd had such wonderful times—anywhere that wasn't a hospital.

But fate had a joke in store for us. Mel's father wasn't well. For three months Mel ran exhaustingly back and forth to another hospital. I pleaded with him not to wear himself out like that, to stop grabbing sandwiches and racing to the hospital, that he needed better nutrition, more rest. He wouldn't listen.

Early in March, Pop died.

A week later, we got the call.

"I have gray news," Dr. Hohlman said. "Gray" isn't supposed to be as bleak as black.

Mel's blood tests were showing an increase in the CEA count, which meant the cancer was back. Not as high as when it began, Dr. Hohlman said. He was "optimistic."

Once again I kept watch through the windows to see him come home; once again had to tell him—"just gray"—news that turned his face haggard, drained hope from his eyes.

So we went back to Co-op Care. To the same rooms and the same faces and the same routine he had hoped he'd said good-bye to forever.

But this time the chemotherapy didn't help. The cancer count climbed higher and higher. We were told there was no point in continuing the treatments. But there was an experimental drug he could be given. This would be in Bellevue Hospital, where NYU has a special wing for these projects. I wouldn't be able to stay with him there, but "hopefully" . . .

This news was given to us the week of June eleventh, our thirty-ninth anniversary.

15

How do you get through the first anniversary alone?

Last year, knowing it would probably be our last one, I wanted us to do something special. A weekend in Bermuda, strolling hand-in-hand along pink sand beaches. A hotel room with balcony doors open to a moonlit sea, while we made the passionate love that hotels evoke in long-married couples.

Reality Check: our last anniversary fell on the day he was scheduled for Co-op Care (for the last time, as it turned out). We walked hand-in-hand, across not sand but concrete, into that all-too-familiar scene. I held his hand again during the blood-taking he always dreaded, went downstairs for the usual Sunday *Times* and irises. "Happy Anniversary," I said, handing him the flowers as he sat waiting for tests, and a hollow-eyed woman beside him stared at us.

Nothing was scheduled for the rest of the day, so we got permission to go downstairs and sit in the courtyard. It was a hot, sunny beach-perfect day. In the middle of the yard there was a two-by-four plot of grass. We climbed over the chain and sat there, while a guard stared at us, trying to decide if we had a right to be there.

"It's not our best anniversary," I told Mel.

"Next year will be better," he said. "For our fortieth, I'll take you to Bermuda."

Sweet optimist, I thought, staring at the emaciated profile, next year will be zero.

I GUESS we would have been flying there this weekend. Instead I'm getting in the car and heading west. To the cemetery. So we can share our anniversary.

Is it still an anniversary if the marriage is over? But it isn't over. I read somewhere that death ends a life, but it doesn't end a relationship.

Nothing's the way you imagine it will be. I had envisioned myself sitting on the stone bench that's at the foot of his grave. But it feels too far from him. What you never imagine is the madness . . .

Who is this insane woman lying on the ground, her arm stretched across the earth above him? "Give me a sign that you know I'm here," she begs. Her fingers are digging into the earth. She wants to dig all the way down to his coffin, pull aside the wooden panel covering his face, smother it with kisses . . .

"The first roses are blooming in our garden."

Silence.

"I promise not to pull up the tiger lilies when I weed, the way I did last year when it upset you so much, remember? I'll bring you one next time I come."

Her fingers try to push deeper into the unyielding earth. "You promised you'd be as close as God permits," she reminds him.

The only answer is a raucous bird perched on the next tombstone.

* * *

THERE WAS mud from the cemetery on the rabbi's shoes when he married us. He had come from an unveiling to join our eager hands "in sickness and in health . . ."

I STAND up, brush the leaves off my clothes, sit on the bench. Taking a tuna sandwich from my purse, I begin to eat, the way we used to picnic on vacations.

"We've had better lunches together, love," I tell him.

EVERYONE ADVISES you to make plans for these days. BE PRE-PARED: a motto for Boy Scouts and widows. So I've made a reservation at my yoga retreat. I go for a long walk in the woods alone, because I can't bear to talk to anyone except him. He's followed me here. I see him standing on the path ahead of me, waiting for me to catch up. He's wearing his yellow jacket. He puts his hand out toward me.

But by dusk I'm sinking. I go up to my room. There's a note on the door: "Flowers at the desk." I run down the three flights, my heart pounding. They're from Mel, he arranged this before he died, how clever, how caring . . .

"Thinking of you," reads the card from our children.

I carry the small basket to my room, weeping in the elevator as people stare. There's an iris in the bouquet.

"Look what the children sent," I tell Mel, the way I did all those times they wired flowers to him at Co-op Care. I throw myself on the bed, crying out over and over again, "Look, Mel, look what the children sent us."

"How DID it go?" the group asks.

"I got through it."

"The anticipation's always worse," says Julie.

* * *

THE GROUP is ending. We agree to meet for dinner once a month. I'm not sorry the group's officially over, because it's still too focused on "poor us."

But it's also invaluable to be able to share what the rest of the world doesn't understand and usually doesn't want to hear. So I ask Joseph if it's possible to go into another group, hoping it will be better. He says there's an ongoing one, which means the people in it are at various stages of bereavement. There won't be the problem of coming in like an intruder where people have already bonded.

Still, I walk in warily. Again, the usual statistics: mostly women (fourteen) to only three men. They're primarily in their fifties and sixties. The same room, the same boxes of Kleenex placed along the table, but instead of raisins the platters hold cookies. Two of the women arrive with cakes. It reminds me of the condolence week. The more upset we are, the more we reach for sweets.

But this group feels very different from the other one. The first moments I'm there, I hear the leader—a vibrant woman named Nedda—telling us that our "challenge" is to find out what our individual strengths are and "learn to capitalize on them."

Muriel, a pretty woman with sorrowful eyes, is describing her husband's unveiling. She had invited forty people. They arrived at the cemetery, but there was something missing: the stone! It hadn't been put up in time.

"What did you do?" we ask, horrified.

Calmly she answers, "I told everyone we'd go ahead with the service and the stone would be there later."

We shake our heads in sympathy, but Nedda zeros in on something else. "Good," she tells her. "You found out how you could be strong!"

So this is the tenor of my new group: not just support for grief, but support for *strength*.

As the weeks go by, I see how different each of us is, even in our common grief. "The ways you react to bereavement reflect the ways you've reacted to other things in the past," Nedda says.

I tell them I'm still running all the time.

"I did, too, at your stage," says a small plump woman named Edna.

But another woman, Sandy, tells me, "At some point you have to stop running and invite the pain in."

"*Invite* it?"

Sandy nods. "Let it become part of you. That's the only way you'll get past it."

Paul, a man who seems to think his brain can control his feelings, has a motto: "Make course adjustments as you go." The women laugh at his super-control, but I like him; he reminds me of the Mel who used to be, before illness forced him to get in touch with every feeling.

An elegantly dressed woman named Reva is the only one in bright colors. But her face has the suffering look of a saint in a Renaissance painting. She sits silent, withdrawn. Then one day we see the trace of a smile.

"Yes," she tells us, wondering at it herself, "it's not that the grief is less, it's that I'm coping more."

One person who doesn't seem able to get past depression is Henry, a man in his late sixties. He seldom takes part in the discussions. One day he bursts out, "The rest of you are luckier than I am. At least you have children."

"That's no panacea," we tell him. "The children have their own lives. Friends are our lifeline."

But Henry doesn't have any friends, either. He and the other men chorus that their wives arranged their social lives, and without that, they're lost.

"You women have it easier," they say. What are we competing for: crumbs?

But it's Sandy I like the most, for the spunky way she shoots down the demon Guilt. I'm telling the group how "late" Mel's unveiling will be, because I'd mistakenly thought it couldn't be before eleven months. Now I find it can't be done in the winter because the ground's too frozen, so it won't be before spring. "He doesn't even have a stone," I tell them. "I feel so guilty about it."

"When are you coming down from that cross?" Sandy asks.

A NEW woman joins the group. Wanting a timetable, she asks, "When will I begin to be myself again?"

"You won't," Nedda tells her. "You become a different person."

A different person. Like a snake shedding its skin?

I call Vanessa in Oregon to tell her my snake analogy. She chooses a more attractive creature to compare me to. "I see you as a butterfly who will emerge from this cocoon."

I buy a coffee mug that has butterflies on it, treat myself to a cloisonné bookmark decorated with gold and blue butterfly wings, hang up a butterfly mobile in the bedroom window.

It's not that I believe in my "chrysalis," but I'm willing to try.

16

"I'm GOING TO try to reclaim my home," I tell Joseph.

"That's a powerful word, 'reclaim.' What does it mean?"

I'm not sure. Exorcise the past?

Home alone tonight, I take out a legal pad. I'll go through the house, making a list of what should be given away.

His bike stares back at me. It's still standing in David's room, waiting for Mel. I have to walk past it each morning. It's got a padlock on it. Why is it locked?

The one he had before was stolen. It was a new bike I'd given him for his birthday. He'd gone off for a ride alone. When the phone rang, I heard his tense voice saying, "They took it!"

It seems he'd gotten a flat tire and was wheeling the bike out of the park. A man stopped him for directions. Mel took one hand off the handlebars to gesture the right way, not realizing there was another man standing behind him—who grabbed the bike and raced off on it, despite the flat tire. "I ran after them," Mel said hoarsely, "but the bastards got away."

"I'm glad you didn't catch them. They might have killed you."

"But they stole it from me."

"It's only a bike. You aren't as easily replaceable."

So I bought him this handsome silver-gray one for our aniversary last year, knowing he wouldn't ride it for long. He insisted on a detachable wheel to make it harder for someone to steal, telling the young salesman, "I intend to have this one for a long time." Then Mel wanted the best lock, a bell, a bag. At each additional request, I felt increasingly resentful. Three hundred dollars from my free-lance money for a bike he'd scarcely use. It's only money, I told myself. But then, it wasn't only the money I was angry about.

Maybe I should sell it, I think, writing "bicycle" on the pad.

"Where did you hide the key?" I ask him.

I make myself open one of his bureau drawers. What should I do with all those neatly folded shirts from the Chinese laundry? His wallet is stuffed with credit cards; don't I have to do something about them? I pick it up; a piece of paper falls out. "Rye bread."

Our bedroom is the hardest room. I should get rid of Mel's bed to make more space. "One of these days," I've been telling friends with a bravado I didn't know I was capable of, "I'm going to redo the bedroom. Get a flowered bedspread, lace curtains." Everyone agrees that's a great idea, the room will look more "feminine." The word destroys me. Do I want it to be "feminine"? Doesn't that italicize that it's for a woman who's alone, no man in her life, her room, her bed?

I go downstairs to the living room. On a three-tier shelf there's a collection of knickknacks from our trips. A small gray elephant made of oyster shells. I see us standing in the bazaar in Hawaii the day Mel bought it; so unusual for him to buy himself anything. "Why *that*?" I said, thinking it was pretty ugly. "Don't you think he's cute?" Mel asked, grinning like a little boy. It can be thrown away now, can't it? I pick it up, dust it with my fingers, gently replace it on the shelf.

Next to it there's an astrological sign on a stand given to Mel by the children years ago. Large letters spell out his zodiac sign:

CANCER. Well, this is one thing I can get rid of. Holding it inside a paper towel as though it's a dead bug, I drop it in the garbage pail. We've had enough "cancer" in this house, I tell God.

At the back of the living room, half hidden on top of a cabinet, is a dusty dark blue box marked SCRABBLE. We used to play every weekend, often ending in a shouting match. "You take so long with every move," I'd complain. "*I* take long!" he'd shout back. We decided to hold "tournaments." The first one to win ten games was to get a silly gift from the loser; mine was an egg-timer so I'd move faster!

Maybe the kitchen's easier. But opening a cupboard, I see that ice-cream maker David gave Mel, who doted on strawberry ice cream. It was supposed to give him something to do when he was ill, but he never used it. "David insists on trying to get me to do things with my hands," said Mel, who had an image of himself as mechanically inept. I guess I should have made ice cream for him. "GUILT," I write in big letters on the pad.

I look in the bathroom medicine chest. Mel's shaving cream is still there. His mouth washes. Those razor blades. I'm seeing him leaning on the sink in despair, when even brushing his teeth took a hundred times more effort than it used to. He was used to doing everything quickly.

"My mother used to brag that I was born in just forty minutes," he told me.

Why did you have to be in such a hurry to die, too?

But the bathtub is starting that slide show going again . . .

NEITHER OF us had been prepared for the horrifying effect the chemotherapy would have on his mind. For two days after the first series of treatments he sat like a robot, staring into space. Then he told me he felt "human" again and was going to take a bath. He liked to soak in long hot Vitabaths, followed by cooling showers. So I didn't think anything of it when he was upstairs for a long time. I was doing the dinner dishes. David, who was visiting that weekend, had gone to his room. It struck me that Mel was taking much longer than usual.

Knocking on the bathroom door, I called out, "Are you okay?" There was no answer.

I opened the door. He was lying slumped against the side of the tub, unconscious, his face gray. Thank God he had let the water drain out! Screaming, I ran over to shake him. There was no response. He's had a stroke, I thought.

I shouted for David, who ran to call Emergency Medical Services.

Groggily, Mel opened his eyes and mumbled, "Why are all the lights out?"

The lights were on.

David and I finally managed to get him out of the tub and into bed. Sirens wailed outside.

"It's the emergency people," David said, racing downstairs to let them in. He came back with two burly men carrying an oxygen canister and stretcher.

"For Pete's sake, what's going on here?" Mel asked.

The EMS men examined him. "His blood pressure's very low. We're taking him to the nearest hospital."

"If he goes anywhere, I want it to be NYU," I said.

"Can't do that, lady."

"Ma," David shouted, "let them do what they want."

I insisted we call Dr. Hohlman.

The operator answering the emergency number said she'd have the physician on standby for the night call us back.

The minutes ticked away.

"They know what they're doing," David kept yelling at me.

"Why are you interfering?" Mel said. I realized he must be feeling better.

When the phone rang, the sleepy voice of the doctor (the elusive Dr. G!) agreed with me that Mel would probably be "best off" in his own bed.

Hanging up, I repeated that to the EMS men.

"Can't take your word for it, lady."

I had to call back, go through the emergency operator again. Dr. G spoke to the EMS men, who put me back on the phone.

"Why did this happen?" I asked.

"You shouldn't have allowed him to take a hot bath," he said. "Chemotherapy lowers the blood pressure."

No one had thought to warn us of this!

The EMS men insisted I sign a release saying it was my responsibility that Mel wasn't being taken to the hospital.

"If anything happens it's on your head, lady."

"Why not? Everything else is."

After they left and Mel fell asleep, a very pale David said he wanted to talk to me. I followed him downstairs.

"Sit down, Ma," my son said sternly.

I sat down and meekly folded my hands in my lap, expecting a lecture.

"Will you promise to do something for me?" David asked.

"That depends."

"I want you to take a CPR course."

I laughed.

"Ma, it isn't funny."

Reaching for my purse, I took a creased three-year-old CPR card out of my wallet. "Care to see this?"

He read it carefully, then handed it back with a look of awe. No article I'd written, no perfect apple pie I'd baked for him, had ever elicited such a look of admiration from my son.

Mel, you would have gotten such a kick out of that story. You loved anecdotes about the children. But I never got around to telling you, because you didn't remember anything about that night.

I YANK open the linen closet where all those dozens of medicines are still stored; grab them and throw them into a garbage bag, not caring that I'm getting hair sprays and suntan lotions mixed up with them.

I march into the bedroom and take down our wedding picture, shove it into his bureau drawer.

"Getting on with life," right?

"Reclaiming," aren't I?

All right, all of you who've been telling me to, where the hell are *you* this long, lonely Saturday night?

17

Everyone seems to be going on vacation. Two by two.

Some of the women are getting around this by going to elderhostels together. The men don't seem to pair up this way. "I'm visiting my wife's relatives," one of the men tells us. "I don't know if they really want me."

"I'm going to California to see my new grandchild," says Edna. "They didn't name him for my husband," she adds.

"Mine *was* named for my husband," says another woman, "but after two years I still can't make myself call the child by his name."

Last summer Mel and I went to Martha's Vineyard. But we felt like aliens among those cheerful vacationers. My most vivid memories of that week are of expensive restaurants, where he'd struggle to get down a few bites.

"Stop watching me," he'd say.

"I'm not," I'd lie.

Once, afraid of bursting into tears in view of the couple laughing at the next table, I escaped to the pink door labeled COMFORT ROOM. Walking back, I was stunned by how lonely Mel looked from across the restaurant. He was hunched over, staring down at the opal ring he loved to wear, as though he was seeing it for the last time. He *knows*, I thought. I hurried back to the table. Looking up at me, he tried to put back the smile he wore for my sake. I took his ice-cold hand in mine and tried to stroke warmth into it. Neither of us spoke, afraid of words.

That was our last vacation.

"HOW AM I going to vacation alone?" I ask Joseph. "I see ads where the scenery's gorgeous, but I can't bear the thought of seeing things he would have loved."

"Vacations are a big issue," he says. "I hear remarks like 'I used to go with my husband' and 'My wife won't be there.' But to deny yourself things like a vacation is to hold yourself back."

I think about taking our trip to Italy and staying with Mel's cousin Ruth. But I'm not ready to go where we would have been together.

Vanessa keeps urging me to visit her. The group encourages me to go.

"I know it sounds crazy," I tell them, "but I feel as if I should stay home and be . . ." I struggle for the right words. "Caretaker of our memories. Know what I mean?"

"Are you doing penance?" Sandy asks.

"From what I understand," says Nedda, "you've paid your dues. You didn't abandon Mel. Aren't you allowed to have *your* life now?"

"I don't know," I say, weeping in front of everyone.

But there's another aspect to this that I don't feel comfortable sharing with the group. I'm afraid of what I think are Vanessa's feelings for me. And I'm afraid of my own neediness.

She calls again, but I hedge. "Do you really expect me to get on a plane and fly across the country alone?"

"And you ride the New York subways?"

"They don't go up that high!"

I ask Ruben for advice. He tells me to be "frank."

I call her back. "There's something I think we should talk about."

"Say on."

"I think . . . I mean . . ." I stop.

"Have we lost contact?"

"What I mean is, I think . . . you want something . . . I mean, more than friendship . . ."

A long pause.

"Anne," she says, "I think of you as a friend whom I love, not as a sexual partner."

"Oh," I say, feeling ridiculous. (For a second I wonder what's wrong with me that she *doesn't* think of me that way!)

"I'm counting on your visit. And I promise"—her voice turns mocking—"to keep my hands off you."

"That's not what I meant. I mean, there's nothing wrong with it . . ." (Oh, God, have I offended her?)

"Anyway, I'm still married to Mel. In my head."

"I get the picture. Come. We'll have a wonderful time."

I'm not sure I believe her. And I'm afraid of flying.

But it's summer and everyone else is going on vacation.

"I'll be there," I tell her.

SHE MEETS me at the airport with a bouquet of flowers. She's wearing a chic dress instead of the usual slacks. The hair she's unabashedly let turn gray is much longer, a stylish bouffant. I feel dowdy and ugly, aware that I've been wearing the same dull clothes for months, embarrassed about the dozen extra pounds from my haphazard eating.

It's an hour and a half drive to her house on the coast. There's a glorious full moon, but by midnight when we reach the shore everything's shrouded in fog.

"Where's your ocean?" I ask, hearing the waves.

"Just forty feet away."

"I've got an insane desire to walk on the beach in the dark."

"Let's do it!"

We scramble down a rocky path by flashlight. She takes my hand to lead me. We walk to the edge of the water, dimly visible.

She waves an arm, owning the sea. "It's so *eternal*."

At the word, I burst into tears.

She puts an arm around me. "Do you prefer to cry standing still or walking?"

I laugh; when did I last hear the sound of my own laughter? We stroll along the edge of the ocean in the fog. She keeps her arm around my waist. It feels wonderful to have an arm around me again.

She takes me on a tour of her house. The ocean's visible everywhere through floor-to-ceiling windows. She's brought the sea inside, too: colorful abstract paintings of the waves, a huge glass jar filled with shells, a whale-shaped piece of driftwood turned into a doorstop. She shows me the room where I'll be sleeping; a bed tidily folds back into the wall. Everything's so organized, so in place, as though waiting to be photographed for House Beautiful. I think of the chaos waiting for me at home.

We go up to the balconied second floor so she can show off her bedroom. It's the opposite of the gray and beige simplicity downstairs. The bed's piled high with flowered pillows, ribboned sunhats strewn artfully on the carpet. On the window seat, a menage of stuffed animals huddles together. I glimpse a needy little girl beneath that assured facade.

The next morning we drive to another part of the coast, where huge waves surge under arches formed from volcanic lava. I run madly into the icy water, trying to get as far as the arches, but the surf pulls fiercely at my legs. I'm barely able to get back.

"I'm very impressed," she says, afraid of the water—like Mel. We sit on the sand, tilting our faces toward the sun. Her hand rests on my bare thigh.

I get back to her house drenched and chilled.

"I need a hot bath," I tell her.

"I'll give you some bubble bath to use. And a candle for atmosphere. How would you like some wine?"

I undress by the light of a candle she's left on the edge of the sink. She comes in with a glass of red wine.

"Enjoy," she says. "I have to take care of the laundry." We're leaving for the San Juans early the next morning.

I lie there in the tub, soaking up the warmth, sipping the wine, feeling cherished. I love her, I tell myself, love the way she cares about me. And an unfamiliar longing goes through me. I've never loved a woman, I think, holding the ruby wine up to the light, but who's to say there's anything wrong with it? *I* have to have someone to love, too.

Besides, the tape in my head runs on, it wouldn't be as much like being unfaithful to Mel as if it were a man.

Wrapping a robe around myself, I go into the kitchen where she's loading clothes into the washing machine.

"My back's killing me," she says. "I don't know what I did to it."

"Want a massage? I learned how to give good ones at my yoga place."

"Sounds great."

We go upstairs to her bedroom. I lie beside her on the flowered bed and rub her back. "That feels good," she says.

After a while, I stop. We lie there silently, listening to the sound of the waves. I could lie like this all night, it's so wonderful to have a body beside me again.

"You better go to your room now," she says, getting up. "I have to put the clothes in the dryer. We're leaving early, so go downstairs and get some sleep."

"Okay," I say after a moment.

Alone in my room, I'm surprised that I'm not upset. What I feel is a kind of triumph. I wasn't afraid to reach out. Is the numbness beginning to wear off?

We drive to the San Juans ferry, ten hours in the car.

"Read to me to keep me awake while I drive," she commands. I pick up the book between us. It's May Sarton's journal, *Solitude*. Beautiful words about being alone and about friendship between women. What happened, I want to ask, was it too sudden a reversal on my part? Or is it that you really *don't* think of me that way? But I lack the courage to say anything.

Arriving at the island late at night, we check into a motel. It has twin beds. It feels strange being here, as though someone's missing. I've never been in a motel with anyone but Mel.

Vanessa goes into the bathroom to shower. I sit on the edge of the bed, homesick and panicky, worrying that the children won't know how to reach me if there's any emergency. I call David to give him the number, thinking it's three hours earlier in Florida, forgetting that time works the other way, so for him it's 2 A.M. There's no answer. "Your mother," I tell his answering machine, "just saying hello. Here's the number in case . . ."

Hanging up, I suddenly remember the time difference! What will David think, that I've lost my mind?

Vanessa comes out of the shower, says good night, gets into her bed, pulls the quilt over her head.

I lie awake, staring into the darkness.

We stay at the San Juans for three days; roam the beaches, binge on ice cream cones, swim in an icy lake in the middle of the woods.

"You have to see my beach bunnies," she says, and takes me to a meadow where hundreds of very small rabbits leap around at sunset.

"Hello, little bunnies," she croons lovingly.

We never talk about what happened.

IT'S THE last day here and we're picnicking on a grassy bluff overlooking the harbor. The day is sunny and warm, the sky an unmarred blue.

"Have you ever done anything you considered brave?" she suddenly asks.

I laugh. "Getting on the plane to come here."

"I've been trying to think of the most courageous thing I've ever done. What would it be for you?"

I stare at a motorboat cutting a white line through the gray water.

"I was brave the other night."

She puts her hand over mine, gently. "You're too vulnerable. It would be . . . clumsy."

We sit there looking at each other, while a screeching gull soars in circles above us.

"So you meant what you said on the phone?"

"It's better this way."

Her palm stays over my hand. I don't move. She's right; it's better this way. What we have is a loving friendship.

I feel reprieved from a kind of insanity.

Maybe someday I'll be able to love again.

18

I'M FACING THE first birthday without him.

A week before, I stop in a jewelry store to buy a new strap for my watch. In one of the cases there's an exquisite pair of gold and blue earrings shaped like miniature harps.

"How much?" I ask.

"Seventy dollars," says the saleslady, holding them up. The light turns them translucent.

"Oh, I can't," I tell her.

But as I leave the store, I think, why can't I? I've never bought good jewelry for myself. If Mel were here, I'd tell him about the earrings and he'd buy them as a "surprise" for my birthday.

Maybe you have to learn to give to yourself.

I go back into the store. "I'll take them," I tell the saleslady. "And I'd like them gift-wrapped."

Taking the small card she hands me, I write on it: *To Anne from Anne with love.* I'll open the "gift" on my birthday.

When I tell the group, everyone applauds.

*   *   *

PART OF this business of learning how to take care of yourself is lining up ways to survive things like birthdays. It's hard for me to ask for help, but friends can't be expected to be mind readers. I tell Dorothy I need to have lunch with her that day. Blanche, the good angel who sent me to Joseph, comes with us. We meet in a charming Greek restaurant, they treat me to lunch, we laugh a lot. "I don't intend to be Ms. Sad Sack," I announce. We drink to that.

In a non-stop marathon to keep from thinking too much, I race from the luncheon to dinner with my therapist friend Judy. She's cooked a birthday feast for us. "Low-calorie," she swears. Then we devour ice cream cake washed down with champagne, giggling like naughty children.

"To you," she toasts.

"To Friendship!" I answer—like a prayer.

How do widows without friends survive?

CAUTION: LOOK out for the roller-coaster. Within days, I've zoomed all the way down again. This bereavement thing isn't like an illness that runs its course, your temperature returns to normal, you're cured.

"It's one step back for every two steps forward," Joseph says.

"With me," I say glumly, "it's *one* step forward and *two* steps back. I still can't get rid of Mel's bed or his clothes. Can't even open his closet door."

"Anne, I've known you for a while now. Believe me, you're taking two steps forward."

Are counselors supposed to apply this kind of verbal Band-Aid?

"You don't understand the pain," I tell him.

"What does it look like?"

"I don't know what you mean."

He points to the extra chair in his office. "Your pain is sitting there. What does it look like?"

I stare at the straight ladder-backed chair. All I can see is my coat thrown over the back. Or is there some kind of shadowy figure, shaped like Mel? I feel chilled, bare across the chest, exposed. I want to hug the pain against me for warmth.

"Maybe," says Joseph, "you don't want to let go of the pain about Mel."

Why should I? It keeps us connected.

MY MIND keeps repeating the digits of Mel's office number like a mantra: 9842305, 9842305, 9842305 . . . We used to speak to each other four or five times a day. And when he was away on trips, he'd call me late at night. Coming home from my writing workshop, I automatically look at the clock on the kitchen wall. Eleven. That's when he'd call. "Hi, honey, how are you? Miss me?"

"Everything you're feeling is normal at this stage," Joseph keeps saying.

"But why *now*? It's worse, not better."

He explains for the umpteenth time that during the earlier months, shock and denial cushion the pain.

"You mean now the anesthesia's worn off?"

"That's a good way to put it."

"Great," I say, hurling the wadded-up Kleenex into his wastebasket.

"Life's a bitch," he says.

Two STEPS back? A hundred! I run back into the past, dreaming about him night after night. The "B.C." days back with a vengeance. He's well, he has a full head of hair, we're making love to each other. I wake up to find my hand groping in the empty bed beside mine. I pull the blankets over my head, trying to find my way back into the dream.

IT'S SATURDAY afternoon. I'm roaming aimlessly around the apartment, unable to make myself go out, incapable of even getting dressed. I know I shouldn't go back to bed, that's a danger sign. But there's such heaviness inside of me. I doze off, lying on my side, with my back to the door.

I sense someone coming softly up the stairs, sitting behind me on the bed, but I don't turn to look. I feel an arm go across my waist. My fingers stroke the familiar hairiness. "Take me back with you," I beg. I can't, he's answering silently. Or is he asking do you really want that?

And I know I don't. A part of me wants to live.

"HALLUCINATION," says Ruben.

I won't believe it. He was here. He came back, for *me*. He does still exist—somehow, in some form.

"Let him go," Ruben says.

"Let go," Joseph echoes.

How *dare* they tell me that?

I stand in our bedroom with my arms wrapped around the air in front of me, as though I'm embracing him. "Are you here?" I keep asking, "are you here?" One day it comes out, "Are you *there*?" as though the distance between us is widening.

Something's been happening with that picture of him that hangs over our bed. His eyes seem to follow me. If I walk to the left, he's looking that way. If I move to the right, his eyes are turned in that direction. It makes me feel as if he's watching over me, trying to send me a message.

I show Dorothy the picture. "Is it a trick of the glass?" I make myself ask.

"Some pictures have that effect," she says.

*   *   *

RUBEN SAYS it's necessary for me to make the transition from Mel as a "presence" to Mel as "memory." But I'm afraid of losing the sound of his voice, losing him over and over again.

"I don't want to do it," I tell Ruben.

He shrugs. "The choice is yours. You can be a mourner for the rest of your life—or begin to put your focus on other things."

I twist my wedding ring, staring down at the carpet.

"Bereaved Anne," he says, "or Anne, who is bereaved."

I understand the difference.

COMING INTO the apartment, I stop myself from calling out my usual, "I'm home."

I don't look out the window to see him coming back at seven.

Instead of opening a can of tuna fish for dinner, I bring in chicken and turn on the oven that hasn't been used all these months.

I force myself to sit at the dining table instead of eating on the couch. The empty chair at the other side of the table stares back at me. To avoid looking at it, I open one of those dozens of magazines still in mailing wrappers. It's the first time I've been able to read.

The subscription to one of those magazines is expiring. LAST CHANCE warns the card. A thought occurs to me. I don't have to renew this subscription if I don't want to, Mel always liked that magazine more than I did. It's my choice now. I repeat that, this time out loud:

"*My* choice now."

Freedom feels strange in my mouth.

But I like that word "re-new."

19

WHAT DO YOU do with the clothes? That's the question that comes up in the group over and over again. Half of the women—and all three men—say they haven't "touched a thing" after nearly a year. But Muriel, the woman who had the unveiling without the stone, says that giving away her husband's clothes "empowered" her.

"I can't decide," I tell them. (We're all finding indecisiveness a problem, maybe because it's so outrageous not to be able to ask the one who's gone, "What do *you* think?")

The children had said they would help with Mel's clothes, but they keep putting it off. "Don't pressure me," David says in a rare outburst. I realize this is too difficult for them.

Dorothy offers to help. "I can be more ruthless with Mel's things than you can," she assures me.

"That's a generous offer," I tell her. "Yes, we'll do it."

"When?"

"Maybe the week after . . . maybe . . ."

Joseph says I'll know when the time is right. How do you know, does an alarm go off?

Seven-and-a-half months today: The group discusses the problem of the clothes again.

"A good question to ask yourself," Nedda tells us, "is whether your actions are helping you move forward or keeping you where you are. Holding on to the clothes may make you feel as if life is still the way it was. You need to acknowledge that it isn't."

I call Dorothy. "I guess I'm ready," I tell her, "or as ready as I'll ever be."

But I don't want his clothes pawed over on a thrift table. I've got to find a home for them. I decide to donate them to Soviet Jews who've immigrated here. Mel would like that; his father was from the Ukraine.

David instructs me to keep the Willie Mays shirt he gave Mel last year. (Mays was an idol of Mel's.) "I'll want the shirt for my son," says David, who doesn't have any children, isn't even married yet. "And save Dad's ties." He used to make fun of his father's taste in ties.

Dorothy arrives armed with a batch of large green plastic garbage bags. We start with the downstairs coat closet. Super-calm, I take out coats and jackets and efficiently go through the pockets. I find scribbed notes: "call Chuck," "pick up milk," "cleaners." Subway tokens. Wads of crumpled Kleenex that I used to scold him about. I see Mel scrounging in his pockets for change, bits of tissue drifting down like snowflakes.

Silently I hand each jacket to Dorothy to put into a bag. She finds four one-dollar bills in a pocket I've overlooked. "You'll get rich this way," I tell her.

But when I get to his bicycling jacket, I put it back into the closet. "Not this." She doesn't ask why. I don't tell her that nights when I come home tired, I hold the gray wool sleeve against my cheek.

We move up to the bedroom, to his bureau. I take out those laundered shirts one by one, hand them to her without a word.

"You're doing very well," she says. I think she's finding this harder than she expected. But when I open the top drawer and see all those bills, notes, cancelled checks, three watches, half a dozen pairs of glasses, I tell her we'll have to leave them for me to tackle by myself. Some other time. Maybe. In the bottom drawer there's an unused box of handkerchiefs with an "M" monogrammed in each corner, a gift from someone or other. I can't think of anyone else whose name begins with M, so I put the box back.

"I guess we'll have to do his closet now," I tell her. "Maybe we should take a break, have lunch first."

"Why don't we just get this over with?" She touches my arm. "Mel wasn't his clothes," she says. "Mel was *Mel*."

But as I open the closet door that's remained closed all these months, I'm not so sure she's right. These things may not be Mel, but they're all I have of him. All those neatly pressed business suits waiting for appointments that won't be kept. I take out each one, ransack the pockets, hand them to her. Farther back, behind these conservative suits, hang the multicolored clothes that were the other side of him. The maroon Grecian shirt with an embroidered border running down the front, that he liked to wear for parties. He looked so self-conscious in it, as though he was never really sure it was all right for him to be wearing it. The orange warmup suit he wore on vacations. He was so diligent about exercise, doing sit-ups every night for the nonexistent potbelly he was sure he was getting. The elegant velour robe I gave him for his last birthday, in burgundy, his favorite color. Why does someone's favorite anything become so meaningful after the person has died?

I run my fingers over the warmup suit, put my hands in the sleeve of the robe. "Not these."

"If this is too hard for you, we can put everything back," Dorothy says.

"And go through this *again*?"

But I'm looking at the Willie Mays shirt.

* * *

WE END up with five bulging bags sitting in the middle of the living room. "Let's get them out of here fast," I tell her. But it's Friday afternoon and the offices close early; why didn't I have the sense to pick another day? Now I have to face those bags all weekend. They look as if there are dead bodies stuffed inside them.

Monday morning I call an office that advertised it's "eager" for men's clothing.

"What size?" asks a bored voice.

"Medium," I tell her.

"We're overstocked on those. Don't you have any large?"

"Sorry, but my husband was medium."

"Well, maybe in a few weeks."

A few weeks! Hysterically I tell her I can't have them here, it's too much for me.

She sighs. "All right, bring them over. They can sit in the hallway with the other stuff."

I hang up and think about Mel's clothes in a hallway, unwanted. I call a place that takes furniture.

"Can you use clothes, too?" I ask. "Clean, pressed."

They don't take even unpressed clothes, the woman tells me apologetically. "But I know a man who just came here from Russia. Do you want his number?"

I call. He barely understands English. I have to repeat the directions over and over again, very slowly. He agrees to come tomorrow night. His voice is gruff. I picture a huge man who will scoff at the mediums, leave without taking them.

He's supposed to come "about five-thirty, yes?" By six, I'm pacing the floor. By six-thirty, I'm cursing myself for not having taken them to that hallway. At ten to seven, the bell rings. I run to the door—and stare through the screen at a man who looks, in the dusk, like Mel! Same height, same width, dark hair. "They'll fit you!" I shout.

I ask him what his name is. "In English," he says, "it would

be Michael." Same initial. I've found a home for the monogrammed handkerchiefs.

He's very appreciative, will take all the clothes. I ask him if
he can use a chair. It's a leather "earth chair" that I can't bear
to look at because Mel sat in it day after weary day near the
end. The man strokes the soft leather. "In my dreams, I have
a chair like this." His family has been sitting on two kitchen
stepladders.

I want to adopt this man, Michael, and his wife who needs,
he tells me, a warm coat, and their twelve-year-old son who
watches too much TV instead of "doing the . . . you know . . .
study." Americanized already? I tell him that when he comes
back for the chair, I'll try to have a coat for his wife, books for
his son.

"How can I thank? You are too kind."

"No, no . . ." But I can't explain (where is the translator who
could turn what I feel into words?) that *I* am the one who's
grateful, because he'll wear Mel's clothes, give them life. I simply
smile and shake hands.

But after he's left (why is it always *afterwards* that I fall apart?)
I find myself on my knees, crying out between wrenching sobs
that hurt my stomach, "Mel, isn't this miraculous?" Convinced
that some mystical force, some guiding angel—"Mel, was it
you?"—sent just the right person here tonight.

A week later, Michael returns for the chair. In the calm of
daylight, I look at his paunchy build and realize he doesn't
resemble Mel at all.

"WHAT DID giving away his clothes do for you?" asks a new
woman in the group. I shake my head, unable to answer. Where
is that "empowerment" I heard about? I feel cheated. Bereft. I
think of that man walking around in Mel's clothes and I want
to tell him to return them. They don't belong to him.

"It's another loss," says Joseph. "But I assure you that getting
rid of the clothes is a positive step."

As the weeks pass, I do begin to feel a sense of something . . . "Empowerment," whatever that may be? I've reclaimed one small part of my home that I was afraid to look at. Like reclaiming one small part of life.

20

I HAVE A habit of seeing Mel beside me in the car, so of course I talk to him. (Not as bad as a woman in the group who automatically gets into the passenger side!)

I'm driving back to my yoga place, but I'm caught in a tangle of traffic, all the people who are "leafing" this glorious October Sunday. Ironic that leaves flame into such brilliant beauty because they're dying.

Remember when we used to go leafing, Mel? Remember those woods in New Paltz, where we would hike for hours, coming home with leaves that I'd vainly try to preserve?

There's no way to keep these memories at bay, not as long as I drive on the same roads we traveled together. I try to avoid every place we were in, but Joseph says that means cutting out half the "possibilities" of my life. Funny to think you never met Joseph. You'd like him.

The car swerves across the dividing line, a driver honking in rage.

"Sorry," I tell you. "I was looking at that turnoff to Copake."

That's where we went the day after our wedding, to work in a summer stock theatre.

Last year we drove past this turnoff, too. We'd driven up this way to see the leaves, but you were too tired to get out of the car and walk. And it was a drizzly miserable day. I wanted to stay somewhere overnight, a final weekend away, but every place had a NO VACANCY sign. SORRY, some added.

"Me, too," I said, trying to make you smile.

Around dusk we started home, depressed from sitting in the car all those hours, staring at the rain. A whole day wasted, when we couldn't afford to lose a minute.

And then, as we passed the turnoff, in an effort to salvage *something*, I asked, "Want to see what Copake looks like now?"

"If you want," you said, not caring.

I turned off the highway and drove down that long curving road past farms with pumpkins staring at us from the posts.

"I wonder if the fountain's still there," you said.

"What fountain?"

"The one in the middle of the square."

"I don't remember any fountain. Are you sure?"

When we got to the handful of stores and one gas station that was apparently the village, nothing looked familiar to me. But you woke up from your lethargy. "There's the fountain," you said. "I told you there was one. And there's where we bought groceries from that man who was always so suspicious of our checks." You got out of the car almost eagerly. "I wonder which way the Grange is." That was the building we'd used for a theatre.

"I don't know, I can't remember any of it." It seemed such a loss not to be able to remember.

"It was down that road," you said. "I'm sure of it."

"This is crazy," I said, following you, amazed at your sudden energy. "It's probably gone."

You had such a look of joy on your face. You used to love theatre. You wanted to act, to direct, to write plays. Why did it all get lost under the urgencies of making a living, raising a family, all the "shoulds" life puts on us? But you made peace with your choices. A week before you died, you quoted Browning to me: *"I regret little, I would change still less."* Enviable, my husband.

I was the one who remained in theatre, an actress for years until motherhood became more important. But that acting training was proving useful now.

"We should vacation here next year," you were saying.

"That would be great," I recited. There were four months left.

"There it is!" you shouted. "That's the Grange."

"Are you sure?"

"I'd know it anywhere."

It wasn't.

"I bet it's that one on the other side of the road," I said, pointing to a white wooden building that looked like a postcard from the past.

"Can't be."

It was.

You put your arm around my shoulder, the way you used to, and kissed me on the cheek. "Pretty smart, aren't you?"

"It's about time you realized that," I said, playing my old role well.

There were a lot of cars parked outside, the sound of music within.

"We shouldn't go in," you said.

I walked around to the side, because I remembered there'd been a door leading into the yard—and there it was, wide open.

"You can't just walk in like that," you called out.

But I was already stepping into that huge kitchen where I'd stood when I was young, newly married, stagestruck. Because it was a cooperative theatre, we'd all taken turns doing everything—including cooking for the whole company, twenty-two hungry actors. Spaghetti, endlessly, because we had so little money. There had been a large black potbellied stove that never heated anything properly . . . But there was one, standing in the corner! Could it really be the same stove, standing like a relic beside a gleaming white electric range?

And there was a long wooden table scratched with initials. But it couldn't be, could it, the same one we'd all sat around, shouting with laughter, arguing about who had "stepped on" whose lines, griping about how the audience had "sat on its hands"? Proudly trying out that new jargon. Certain we were all going to be stars.

A woman in a waitress's uniform, little white apron and all, came through the swinging door and stared at us.

"We didn't mean to intrude," I told her. "But we worked here a long time ago. It used to be a theatre. We just wanted to see it."

She shrugged. "Go in if you like."

Pushing open the door, we found ourselves in the midst of a reception that seemed to be ending. People were walking back and forth holding wraps, calling out good-byes. A heavy man weaved past us, balancing two long-stemmed glasses, ignoring the champagne spilling on the wooden floor. On what used to be our stage a boy was gathering up tapes, as some deafening song blared over the room.

Then I saw the bride. She must have been about eighteen. Her face was clear and unlined; her white satin dress gleamed in the lights. She was chatting with a few guests, holding out her left hand to show them the new ring, knowing how beautiful she looked and how enviable. A young man in a tuxedo put a possessive arm around her waist and whispered something. Laughing, she leaned against him.

"Back in a minute," I mumbled to Mel.

I locked myself in the Ladies' Room—pink walls, pink soap, pink hearts-and-flowers paper towels—and splashed cold water into my eyes.

I found Mel standing alone in the bare cubicle that had been the box-office, where he'd written press releases when he had a strong young body and laughed a lot. The face he turned toward me was haggard. "Let's get out of here."

I took his hand. It felt icy. We walked through the crowd that was oblivious to us, as though we were invisible, wrapped in our black raincoats. We're messengers of death, I thought, who have invaded their celebration.

"REMEMBER?" I ask the space beside me in the car.

21

"Is it better to be the one who dies or the one who has to go on?" That's what comes up in the group now.

The vote goes to the "lucky" one who's died.

Even Sandy's been in a funk. "I'm in cement," she keeps saying. But today she comes in eager to tell us something.

"After one of those isn't-worth-living weekends," she says, "I made an appointment so I'd have to get out. But as I got to the subway, the doors closed in my face. I thought, *nothing's* going right for me anymore. I was drowning in self-pity."

That night Sandy turned on the TV and heard about a train that had caught on fire, hundreds of people injured. It was the train she had missed!

"It sure makes you realize," she says, "you do want to live, after all."

"Bereavement," Nedda tells us, "brings up old issues."

I've made a dinner date with a friend to fill Saturday night.

At the last minute, she cancels. No one else is free. I'll be alone. The familiar panic sets in, a thickness in my throat. I feel as if I'm choking. The child in me who used to be left alone too much takes over.

This is what is meant by an "issue."

There's an even bigger one. I've always been afraid that if I love someone that person will leave me.

He has.

"Abandonment," says Joseph, giving voice to the unutterable, "that's what this is all about."

In the journal that you don't show anyone, where you confide the craziness, the unsharable thoughts—that frightened child crouching inside of you—you find yourself writing:

> Coming home tonight, I groped in the dark for the light switch. That's how I feel about my life—groping for the light, for the stairs, no one caring if I fall, no one hearing if I call out . . .

I draw a large black X through the words. In capital letters, I write: "THE MOST DANGEROUS ENEMY IS SELF-PITY."

DAVID COMES for a visit—all of two days. It's overwhelming to have another human being in the apartment again, to hear the phone ringing for someone else, footsteps running up the stairs, the stereo blaring. I warn myself not to clutch at him, but make the mistake of asking if I can ride with him to Washington, where he's going for a job interview. He looks away, uncomfortable.

"Don't you have work to do?" he asks.

"You're right," I lie.

He's twenty-nine, has his own life, doesn't want Mama tagging along. It isn't my children's function to fill their mother's loneliness.

"I'm not the most important person in anyone's life anymore," says a woman in the group.

"What are you going to do about it," says Sandy, "build a monument to that?"

The reality is that you're not a wife anymore. Nor are you a mother, in the old sense of being central to your children.

"I feel as if I'm between lives," I tell Joseph, "in some kind of abyss."

"What are you going to do to fill it?"

They're clever with the questions, these therapists.

Joseph's getting tougher with me. He gives me an assignment: to describe where I hope to be a year from now.

I stare at the blank page, unable to do my homework.

He gives me another assignment: to list my needs and how I plan to get them met. After I dutifully do this, I see that my "needs" read more like "should's":

Need to stop running so I can stand still long enough to write again

Need to see only positive people who won't pull me down each time I try to get up

Need to stop being comatose in front of the TV

Need to start eating decent meals

Need to stop looking like a Bag Lady

Need to get rid of Mel's bed (???)

When I finish, I realize I've omitted something from my list of needs. Love.

Whenever I think about making a date to see someone, it's invariably a woman. Is half the world's population ruled out because I'm a widow?

Paul, that man in the group who reminds me of Mel, seems so attractive. I wish I could ask him if he'd like to meet for dinner, the way I so easily ask the women. But I come from the generation that believes men do the asking. My feminist daughter would hoot if she knew.

Anyway, how would I explain to this nice man that it's just companionship, just an interesting conversation, a pleasant evening, that I have in mind?

Or is it?

I'M GETTING paranoid about men.

I'm on Amtrak, coming back from another visit to my sister. A middle-aged man with a pleasant face sits beside me on the crowded train. I'm frantically searching through my purse for the ticket, juggling a paper cup of water in my other hand. The man says something. I look up. In broken English, through some kind of heavy accent, he's offering to hold the cup for me.

"I can hold it myself," I snap.

The train slows as it gets to a station. My suitcase is stored in a space behind the seats. I twist myself around like a pretzel, to make sure it's not stolen as people crowd past. But that man is standing up, too.

"I help?"

"No!"

Abashed, he sits back down, shrinking away from me. He's probably a visitor to this country, lonely. I stare into the window beside me. In the dirty pane, I can see my face: tense, angry, ugly. Why is he bothering me? How can he even be interested, the way I look? Leave me alone, don't you see that I'm untouchable? Half dead.

I START thinking about taking off my ring. Walking in a park strewn with fallen leaves, I say out loud, "On the anniversary of his death I'll move the ring to my right hand." Suddenly I'm sprawling on the ground. I brush dead leaves off my slacks, rub my bruised knee, thinking how strange that I fell just when I was saying that about the ring.

If just the *thought* of moving it to my other hand can trip me up, how can I ever have a relationship with another man? How could I even ask that man in the group to have dinner with me?

"Just think of it as dinner," says Joseph. "Not the big R-word." But Mel's wife isn't ready.

22

HERE WE GO into the Obstacle Course known to normal people as the holiday season.

"Come for Thanksgiving," says my friend Edie. (Ever since that awful Passover, she's practically adopted me.)

"Thanksgiving? I'm back somewhere in July!" All year I've been in this strange time warp, never sure what day—or month—it is. I'd like to skip this whole season. Is there some way to hibernate until it's over?

At the Thanksgiving table, surrounded by Edie's family, I feel an emptiness that the food I'm devouring doesn't seem to fill. As alienated from the laughing people around me as though they're speaking a foreign language.

Suddenly I feel a hand stroking the back of my head. It's what Mel used to do in social gatherings as a silent hello. I turn around; no one's there. But as I turn back to the table, I feel that hand again, stroking my hair. And for a second time, I have the overwhelming feeling that he's with me.

Today I'm too needy to care that I may be "disturbing" Mel's rest.

NEDDA SAYS we have to learn to be "self-starters." So instead of waiting for people to take pity on me, I'll do the inviting. I'll give my first dinner party and invite our three oldest friends, who go all the way back to college days: a couple named Elaine and Kenneth, and the perennial bachelor of our diminishing circle, Charles. They're almost all who are left of our group. Time is catching up with us: four deaths within the last few years. The latest one—before Mel—was Townsend Brewster, the poet and playwright. Last Thanksgiving, Townsend was exuberant because he'd been appointed resident poet at a New Jersey college. His first week there, crossing a campus road at night, he was struck by a car, killed instantly. (When Mel heard the news, he said, "Instantly? Lucky man.")

I'm trying to move forward with this dinner party, but old friends bring up the past. Elaine has a habit of resurrecting our college days, when we all worked together in an acting company some students had formed off-campus. That's how Mel and I met, when I was eighteen.

He'd already graduated, but was invited back to direct Strindberg's *The Father*. I was in another play at the time, even busier playing tragic heroine *off*-stage because I'd just broken up with a boyfriend. One of my friends said, "I want you to meet someone who's just right for you." She gestured toward the skinniest boy I'd ever seen, a dark-haired scarecrow intently leaning forward in a chair as he called out directions to his cast. We were introduced during a break in the rehearsal, but I have no recollection of what we said. How can I have lost that? All I remember is telling my friend afterwards, "Never in a million years!" It became a joke with us.

Raising my glass in a toast, I debate: *To those who are missing*. Revise to: "Here's to friendship." I can't afford to cry, I have to serve the dinner.

I used to get so frazzled before guests arrived, even with Mel helping me. But tonight, doing a solo job, I'm untypically calm—as though it all doesn't matter. The gourmet Chinese chicken has been timed to perfection (amazing that I haven't forgotten how to cook!). I didn't even forget to chill the wine. "See how efficient your wife's become?" I ask Mel.

Teasing Charles, Kenneth says, "Do you know the difference between eating and dining?"

"This dinner," says Charles, who has an Old World courtesy, "is dining."

"Right," says Kenneth. "But there's one thing missing."

"I know," I say apologetically. "Candles." There's no way to explain to someone like Kenneth, who likes conversations to be kept on the Noel Coward side, that I can't be—cannot bear to be—*too* festive.

"This is my first dinner party," I tell them. They pretend not to understand.

Elaine veers into, "Remember . . . ?" Quickly I steer the conversation to politics, knowing my liberal friends will keep it going full steam from there. Righteously we vent our rage at Bush and Quayle; easier than God.

Under cover of the political argument on the other side of the table, I ask Elaine, who's got a good sense of decorating, "Won't the living room look more spacious if I take that removable hutch off the cabinet?" I don't tell her I suggested this to Mel, but he always hated the thought of moving furniture. "It looks fine the way it is," he'd say—about *everything*.

"It would look better," Elaine agrees.

Feeling shamelessly manipulative, I say, "I'm going to pay the maintenance men to move it for me."

"You've got two men right here who can do it," she says—as I hoped she would.

Charles and Kenneth leap to the task as though it's a lark. "Thanks for the after-dinner exercise," says Charles. But when they lift off the hutch, I stare at the opened-up space in panic. What would Mel say? It's the first change in the apartment.

As they leave, Elaine whispers, "We think you're adjusting beautifully."

I feel like screaming at her, you don't see me in the middle of the night.

Closing the door, I turn to face the silence.

"Want to do the dishes?" I call up the stairs. Mel liked washing dishes; it "soothed" him, he'd say. I see him hurrying down the stairs in his old yellow terry robe, always careful to change clothes first.

The evening was successful, I tell myself. But there's no one to talk it over with. I pour another glass of wine. But if I start down that road, I'll be a mess in the morning. Instead, I leave all those dishes and go to bed. One advantage to living alone is that no one's bothered if you leave dishes until the morning. And you're not keeping anyone awake if you cry in bed.

A CHRISTMAS catalogue arrives in the mail, red and green lettering on the cover promising: "GIFTS FOR THE MAN IN YOUR LIFE."

"A hard time of year for everybody," Joseph reminds me. I bet *he* doesn't celebrate alone.

I'm facing Chanukah, the candle-lighting time when we all used to be together, when we were a Family. Last year the children came.

"Care for a game of handball?" David asked Mel. They always played handball together when David visited, the way they used to when he was a child.

Mel sat hunched over on the sofa. "I can't," he whispered hoarsely, sores in his throat from the chemotherapy. "I'm sorry," he said, putting his hand over his face to hide the tears, "sorry . . ."

David sat beside him, memorizing his father's face.

"There's nothing to be sorry about," David said.

(A week before Mel died, David wrote to him:

I watched you struggle up those steps, your hands gripping the rails, and I knew that was how I wanted to struggle when I have lost all strength and my children are watching me and don't want to see me so weak, but also want to see me struggle on. Your determined fight means as much to me as the five touchdowns we watched a very healthy Joe Montana throw. The most unfair thing I ever heard you say was in the hospital, when you said you weren't a hero. But that was before you made it home, and struggled up and down those steps, up and down, again and again—and again.)

This year the children aren't coming. I can't cope with lighting the candles alone.

"I'm going to ignore Chanukah," I tell Joseph.

"How are you going to ignore your feelings about it?"

He's beginning to sound like Ruben.

I get one of those phone calls that always seem to come at a pivotal time. It's from the social worker at the hospice, inviting me to a memorial service for everyone who died there during the year.

"It would be too hard for me to attend a service for my husband," I tell her.

"It's for you, too," she says. "His pain is over, but yours is continuing." I'm so moved I can barely answer. It makes me realize how few people really understand.

I agree to come, and tell her I'd like to donate a few items that might be helpful to other patients. Can she use three Marilyn Monroe movies that Tamar videotaped for Mel?

"Oh, our patients would love them!"

When I turn the corner and see that gray stone building again, I have to walk the other way until I'm able to feel numb. How do you feel numbness?

I walk into a large room, carrying a shopping bag of books

and tapes. Sister Mary Loyola, the jovial nun I remember so well, greets me eagerly.

"Are you the Marilyn Monroe lady? God bless."

It's a very small gathering; I guess the majority of people couldn't face coming. Men and women of varying ages, even some children. I smile at a little girl who looks about four. She stares back at me somberly, the expression on her face too old for so small a child.

The service begins with a prayer of St. Francis'.

"Grant that I may never seek so much to be consoled as to console . . ." (A good philosophy for dealing with one's children!)

Sister Mary Loyola asks us to look at the cover of the program we've each been handed. "I drew the picture," she says, "and tried to make it fit what you must be feeling."

The childish drawing shows both a Christmas tree and a menorah—but only half of each.

"Half," she says, "because of what's missing for you." She points out the yellow crayon around the lights. "That's for the glow that comes from remembering."

Then—in this Catholic hospital—a young man playing a guitar leads us in a Chanukah song! It was written by Peter Yarrow of Peter, Paul and Mary. Trying to follow the printed words we've been given, I find myself singing with him:

"Light one candle for the strength that we need, to never become our own foe . . ."

I hear people around me joining in, see the shining faces of the Sisters as they raise their voices exuberantly.

"What is the memory that's valued so highly," we all sing together, *"that we keep it alive in that flame?"*

A FEW nights later, I light the first Chanukah candle.

23

How STRANGE TO be going into a year that Mel will never know.

We spent last New Year's Eve waiting for a hospital bed to be available for him.

He'd been sliding downhill fast, barely able to even drink water without throwing up. Dr. Hohlman suggested that a tube be inserted into the liver to drain it. Hopefully, this "procedure" would help Mel regain his appetite. And he believed it when the surgeon told him the stay would be just a few days.

But the tube wouldn't drain properly—and the "few days" dragged into weeks.

Then, finally, Mel began talking death.

"I just want this to be over," he said wearily, lying there attached to a degrading plastic bag to hold the bile from a tube that stubbornly refused to be capped. "You'll have to accept the way I feel," he said, closing his eyes against any protest.

I stared through the windows at Co-op Care across the courtyard, and blurted out that we should choose a cemetery plot.

"It's for *both* of us," I assured him. "I want to be beside you."

126

"That's nice," he said. As if we were planning our next vacation.

How do you choose a cemetery? It's not like going to Bloomingdale's and picking out dishes. We'd always scoffed at people who prudently make "arrangements" for "that time." We never wanted to think about it. Once Mel's father phoned to say there was space available in the family plot.

"That was a hostile thing to tell us," I said to Mel.

"He just wants the family to be together."

I didn't understand then.

I came up with two choices: that New Jersey cemetery where both his parents were by then (his mother had died years ago) or the Long Island one where my grandparents are buried. As if it was a choice between his family and mine.

"It doesn't matter," Mel muttered. "You decide."

He was released from the hospital, tube still uncapped. I was given the terrifying responsibility of suctioning it and cleaning the wound each day. Grimly leaning over the bed with needles and antiseptic and gauze, I told myself I better check out the cemeteries. But without his knowledge, because once he was safely home he thought he might make it after all.

On a pretext of picking up work, and with Herb willing to stay with Mel, I drove to New Jersey.

Turning into the winding driveway of Riverside Cemetery, I made mental notes: a park-like setting, huge oak trees, birds chirping even in the wintry bleakness—he'd like that. On the other hand, I thought, trying to be a careful shopper, it's a very old cemetery, did it look crowded?

Then I went to inspect the Long Island one. This was much more impressive. (Who is it we think will be impressed?) I was seeing the manicured grounds, neat rows of identical monuments, handsome brick building that housed the offices, versus the plain wooden structure at the other cemetery. MT. ARARAT, read a large sign.

And suddenly it struck me—Mt. Ararat! Where Noah's ark landed.

Mr. and Mrs. Noah. That's who Mel and I were—in that college theatre company's production of Obey's *Noah* soon after we met. We had to sprinkle cornstarch into our dark hair to whiten it, draw lines on our faces, stoop our hungry young bodies into a semblance of infirm old age. And that's how we fell in love . . .

I leaned against a stranger's tombstone and wept.

I came back from the cemeteries unable to decide and called David. (By then I'd had to be frank with the children about the prognosis.)

"It's up to you, Ma," David said. "Tamar will tell you the same thing." Then he called back. "Won't New Jersey be more convenient for visiting?"

I drove to each cemetery again, timing the trips, checking the mileage, to see which was more "convenient." There was, I calculated, a ten-minute difference. I stared at my mileage statistics, then tore them up. How often would I visit anyway? What would I do in that future I couldn't—didn't want to—see clearly, make a habit of visiting Mel's grave?

"The truth is," said Ruben, "you don't want to pick *any* plot. You don't," he informed me, "want Mel to die." For this, I thought bitterly, I'm paying eighty dollars a session?

Determined to do some rational comparison shopping, I drove to each one again. At Riverside there was space available right across from his parents. But would Mel want to be with them? I wished I could ask him. There was a white stone bench at the foot of where a grave could be. I could sit there when I visited him.

But back at Mt. Ararat, I saw how indisputably more luxurious the ambience was. Didn't Mel deserve "the best"—whatever that is? The same feeling that attacks us when we have to choose a coffin, a stone.

A guide showed me plots that were available; four-grave ones only.

"I just need two," I said.

"You can use the other two for your children, or invite some relatives."

Yes, I thought madly, we could all be together.

Frantic, I insisted that Ruben tell me what to do. Discarding psychology for economics, he asked which was cheaper. I explained that Riverside was a "bargain," only two hundred dollars for both graves because that whole section had been bought by a group of immigrants from Mel's father's Ukrainian village. Mt. Ararat, on the other hand, would cost four thousand dollars.

Ruben shrugged. "Put your money into life, not death."

That's when Mel's brother Norman and his wife Gladys arrived from Ohio. I confided in them. Norm offered to go to Riverside with me to help me decide. A brave offer, since his first wife is buried there. We concocted alibis for Mel and left Gladys to "baby-sit."

At Riverside, Norm courteously pointed out all those relatives I'd been so shy about meeting when Mel and I were going out together. Silently, Norm rested his hand on the stone that stood over the grave of his young wife.

"It's very peaceful here," he said.

I showed him where I'd want Mel to lie, in front of the bench.

"So that decides it?"

"Yes," I said doubtfully. "No. I have to check out the other one again." There was a new thought running through my head: Mel couldn't die until a plot had been bought, so as long as the decision wasn't made . . .

The next day Norm stayed with Mel, while Gladys and I ("going shopping, Mel") went to Mt. Ararat.

"Isn't this an impressive setting?" I asked Gladys. Please, make the decision for me.

"The stones look uneven in places," she said. "Is it me or is there something wrong with the ground?"

It's near the ocean, I think. (It isn't.) Were tides surging under Long Island, eating away at the bodies? I felt I was losing my mind.

Gladys and Norm went back to Ohio; I continued obsessing.

Then in February, Dr. Hohlman let Mel know it would be, at most, a few months. Mel started telling me what kind of funeral he wanted.

"If you're talking funeral," I said hysterically, "I want you to know I've been checking out the cemeteries."

"You have?" he asked, impressed.

"I can't choose! Help me." He knew me so well, knew that indecision was *my* illness.

And I asked him if he would ride out to Mt. Ararat with me! (He'd already seen Riverside, too many times.) "It's a beautiful day for a drive," I said. "It will do you good to get out of the house." Sane, I would never have done that to him.

He agreed to go. I had to dress him in his warm jacket, pushing his arms through the sleeves one at a time as though he were a baby; put a warm cap on his head. I had to keep my arm around his waist to support him as he slowly walked to the car, barely able to move one foot in front of the other, more frightened of falling on the pavement than of seeing a cemetery.

"Forget it," I said after a few steps. "It isn't worth it."

"We'll go," he mumbled, "if it will help you decide." I guess he preferred that to having to listen to me agonize over a decision one more time.

So we drove there and he did, in a strange way, enjoy the ride, the getting out of the apartment for a while. The sun was shining, the sky flawless, it was warm enough to have the windows open and the breeze blowing in our faces. Riding out on Long Island as though we were shopping for the country house we'd always talked of buying and never had.

But when I turned the car into the gates of the cemetery, he was silent.

"See how nice this is?" I asked, feeling sick at having brought him there.

He stared at the monuments lined up in mathematically precise rows and made the decision for us in one second:

"Too regimented."

"But don't you think . . . ?"

"Let's get out of here!"

I turned the car around so hastily it almost struck a grave-stone. "I'm sorry," I told him, "I had no right to put you through this."

"It's all right," he said.

But I couldn't stop crying, the car weaving dangerously.

"Honey," he said gently, "it's all right."

No one else will ever be so accepting of my craziness.

24

WHAT DIFFERENT WAYS we each have of handling this. I'm at the monthly dinner with the first support group. It seems to have split into two factions. One half is still focused on how "rotten" everything is.

"This life is so damn lonely," Tess tells me. "Don't you find it that way?"

"I try to keep busy," I start to say.

"I do, too. I'm taking bridge lessons. But it doesn't mean a thing. I'm dead, you know? Dead."

I move to another table, as if she might infect me.

Penny whispers, "Tess may say she's dead, but I notice she's wearing a new leather miniskirt."

We're all clinging to each other as if we're drowning. I should stop coming to these dinners; mutual widowhood isn't enough of a reason for friendship. But I seem to have a hard time letting go of *anything*. Two of the group have dropped out.

"They don't want to be reminded," says Rhoda. She makes it sound like an accusation.

How can two support groups be so different? Is it something that filters down from the kind of leader each one has? I think gratefully of Nedda's toughness when anyone gets too self-pitying; her insistence on finding ways to be "strong."

And I think of some of the people in her group, like Reva, that elegant woman who seemed paralyzed by depression the first time I saw her. Yesterday she told me, "I'm not going to be a widow anymore."

"You mean you're getting married?"

"No way! What I mean is I've decided I don't have to wallow in widowhood, I can be *me*."

But half of Group Number One seems to think that a man *is* the answer, frantically searching for that magical Mr. Someone who will make them whole again. Some of the women admit they've been going to singles bars, but without much success.

"Everyone else there is younger, prettier and more liberated," Penny's been complaining.

It's legendary how widows complain that their friends' husbands make passes at them. But in the safety of the group, a few of the franker women confide how *they* look at the husbands. "I was eyeing my best friend's husband and thinking he was more attractive than I'd realized," says one of the women. "I felt like telling her, if you're a real friend you'll share him with me." She tries to laugh.

Tonight Penny drops a bombshell: she's found "the most wonderful guy." Her eyes sparkle as she reports this success. She looks years younger, has she had a face-lift? Still, he's a dozen years younger than she is—and married. Under her flashing smile, her 'Girls, this is great,' I think I see desperation. It frightens me; I'm never sure I'm not looking into a mirror.

But is it any better to be a reflection of Madge? She's telling us that after a year and a half she still hasn't given away any of Jack's things. "And I still talk to him all the time."

It reminds me of something Nedda said, that we edge back into life at different rates. "It's the way people go into the ocean," she told us. "Some hesitate until they get used to the cold, others plunge."

"I plunge," I said.

"You do?" asked Sandy skeptically. "You sure don't plunge into decisions!"

"I guess I'm less afraid of water," I said, laughing. "I even tried scuba diving after just one lesson."

Everyone was staring at me.

"Well," Nedda said, "it seems there's a very different Anne beneath the one we've been seeing. When is she going to come out?"

That "other Anne" feels very far away in this restaurant to-night. I sit here wishing that just once we could talk about something besides IT.

As THE saying goes, be careful what you wish for.

A waitress runs into the room, screaming, "We just bombed Baghdad!"

I race home frantically, in a taxi to save precious minutes. I have to call my draft-age son, make sure he's all right; have to be at home to watch this horror, as though Mel will be there to put a protective arm around me, reassure me we're not all going to be blown up.

It's the first time since he died that I've watched the news, read a paper, even known what's going on in the world. But without him, I feel totally unprotected.

We all seem to feel the same way, as if our safety net is gone. Reva tells me, "When I heard those sirens wailing as the first Scuds fell on Tel Aviv, I was sick with terror. It brought back my childhood in Europe during the war. I needed my husband so badly I thought I'd die."

WHEN THE cease fire is announced, I weep. "Crazy to cry," I tell Reva, "but there's a whole piece of history we've lived through that Mel never knew about."

"Yes," she says, "the world's changing fast. And our husbands aren't part of this new one."

25

What bizarre shopping expeditions widowhood entails. Now it's a tombstone.

In the hospice, I told Mel what I planned to have inscribed on his stone: HUSBAND, LOVER, POET.

"How nice," he said, blurred by morphine. Still that touch of imitation normality: "Nice." As though I'd told him what book I was giving him for his birthday.

I can't remember whether I told him we'd have a double stone. That's what I envisioned, the Mr. & Mrs. kind, with his epitaph on one side and a blank space for mine on the other. But now the thought of a tombstone waiting for my name upsets me.

"I don't want a stone waiting for me," I tell Joseph.

"There's a stone waiting for all of us."

Well, yes. But it doesn't have to be *up*, does it?

I tell Penny about my dilemma. She says, "I was going to have a double stone, but my son objected. He said, 'It's like you're waiting to fall into the grave with Dad.'" Leaning over, she whispers, "Don't do that double stone bit, honey."

I call *my* son, hoping for similar words because they'll absolve me. David comes through. "I agree with that woman. Tamar and I will take care of your stone when the time comes."

So he's taking that bit of guilt off my shoulders. But when I think about a single stone just for Mel, I feel as if I'm abandoning him.

Ruben suggests I compromise by putting up a family stone with the last name, and a foot marker. But a marker lying flat on the ground seems cold to me. Listen, I tell myself, if the poets in Westminster Abbey just have foot markers, why shouldn't Hosansky? He'd be amused by the thought. But I can't decide. I keep waking up in the middle of the night, staring at tombstones.

Ruben gives me the name of a monument maker, a Mr. *Silverstone*. Did he borrow the name for the job? When I call, I hear the velvety, sympathetic voice of monument makers and morticians. He makes an appointment to come to the apartment with "samples."

When he arrives—looking like a bespectacled, fatherly grocery clerk—he opens his attaché case and takes out two small, flat, rectangular stones.

"Do you prefer polished or unpolished?" he asks, placing the stones side by side on the dining room table. I choke up. Mr. Silverstone clears his throat and looks away. I need to think about this, I tell him.

"Of course," he says. "Of course."

But double, single or family style? Mr. Silverstone takes out a pocket calculator and estimates costs. Trying to appear rational, I get a legal pad and write down the statistics he's reciting. None of them make sense to me, but I nod as if I understand. Everything seems incredibly expensive. What does register is that the family stone with a foot marker is two thousand dollars more than a single stone. Mr. Silverstone takes out a handful of color photos, like a proud grandparent. These are pictures of the monuments other people seem to have been able to choose.

I need time to think about all this, I tell him again.

"Of course, of course."

He leaves the samples for me to consider.

When the door closes behind him, I yell, "Damn it, Mel, *you* make this rotten decision." I need advice, counsel, words. I call David; hadn't he told me he'd have "no problem" dealing with this? He's not in. I leave an urgent message. I try Tamar. The usual busy signal. Sonia. Her recorded announcement lets me know they're "not available." "This is your sister," I tell her machine, "not in good shape." I try Dorothy. The phone rings and rings while I stare at the two stones on the table. No answer. Is the whole world out, busy, disconnected? I curse Herb for having turned his back on me; why isn't he here to help? It's his brother. Brother! I dial Norman. To my surprise, a live voice answers.

Norm says, "All I can tell you is that we plan to have a double stone for ourselves. A single stone seems lonely."

I see the stone standing up over Mel's grave, alone, reproachful.

"But the Orthodox tradition about a double stone," Norm continues, "is that you're saying you won't remarry."

I utter what's more or less a laugh. "I not only don't intend to remarry, I can't even imagine loving again." I'm shocked to realize I'm not sure I mean what I'm saying.

I try to reach Tamar again. For a change, her line isn't busy.

"I'm standing here," I tell her, "looking at two sample tombstones."

She giggles. "Like kitchen tiles?"

"Precisely what I was thinking." I giggle, too. It's an unexpected moment of rapport.

Trying to sound in control of myself, I discuss polished versus unpolished. "Daddy would want it simple," I tell her. "Unpolished."

"Maybe," she says doubtfully, "but he always liked the look of polished stones."

I put a question mark on the legal pad.

"Do you prefer Mel or Melvin?" I ask, pencil poised efficiently above the pad.

"Mel, because that's the way he had it on the masthead of the magazine."

"Good thinking!" I don't want to get off the phone, we're so united, briefly, by all of this.

David returns my call. But the one who had said "no problem," just says irritably, "You decide, Ma. I'm tired."

It strikes me that he's always "tired" when he has to deal with his father's death.

I put the samples into my tote bag and carry them to the support group. (Show-and-Tell time?) When I place them on the table, everyone flinches.

But Henry, who's usually too submerged in depression to join in discussions, picks up the stones and examines them with great interest.

"I can tell you that the polished will keep cleaner," he says. "The unpolished is porous, so it picks up all the dirt, especially if there's much greenery around."

"That's very helpful," I tell him.

But double, single, family? "Can't decide," I say, unable to keep the hysteria out of my voice.

"Why don't you put up a foot marker in the shape of a book, since he liked to read?" someone suggests. I try to imagine Mel's reaction. Would it read, THE END?

I go to Joseph. "Norm says a single stone is lonely."

"A stone isn't 'lonely,' " he says. "But we're not really talking about stones, are we?"

"We're not?"

"Choosing the stone is a big issue for everyone, because it brings up thoughts of one's own mortality."

I don't want to hear it.

I keep asking Ruben what I should do. "Toss a coin," he finally says. He fishes a quarter out of his pocket.

"It isn't that simple, don't you understand?" (Why the hell *don't* you, what am I paying you for?)

On a freezing Sunday, I drive to the cemetery. I tell myself I'm going there in order to see what the other monuments in the section look like. But I know why I'm really going; so I can ask Mel.

"Which one should I pick?" I ask the small tag on a stick barely visible through the snow.

"Honey," I hear him saying, "it doesn't matter."

That's what he used to say when I asked his advice about everything—furniture, vacations, dates. "It doesn't matter that much." I don't like remembering that I used to get angry at him about that.

Back in the group, I bring up the stone again, amazed by everyone's patience.

"The real issue," says Nedda, "is that a stone is an exclamation point for the fact that he's died."

Leaning toward me, she looks straight into my eyes.

"Mel is gone," she says. "He isn't coming back."

The words slap me in the face.

". . . *gone . . . isn't coming back,*" she repeats in the hushed room. "*Never coming back.*"

Shut up, I want to scream, you're lying.

And I realize what this is all about.

"Separation," says Ruben. "That's what the single stone means to you."

"I guess so, because I feel that if we're buried under a double stone, we'll still be together. I have this image of reaching out through our coffins to hold his hand."

"You and Mel will never again touch each other the way you did. But that has nothing to do with stones."

"You don't understand . . ."

"It's psychologically better for you to pick a single stone, because it's absolutely necessary for you to separate from Mel."

He hands me three pieces of paper and tells me to draw a picture of each stone. The pen shakes in my hand.

Taking my sketchy drawings, he shuffles them like a pack of cards and holds them out face down.

"Choose one," he says.

"That's no way . . ."

"Choose!"

My hand reaches, hesitates, pulls out a paper.

I turn it over.

It's the single stone.

I tell Mr. Silverstone that I'll be coming down to what he calls his "showroom."

"Make sure you don't go alone," warns the group.

Unable to ask outright, I scatter hints. Dorothy, my guardian angel, volunteers to go with me.

I make a date with Mr. Silverstone for a week from Thursday. Valentine's Day.

26

It was last Valentine's Day when Dr. Hohlman told Mel the treatments weren't working.

I had forgotten it was Valentine's Day. All I knew was that I had to get Mel to the doctor's office for his checkup. By then, he was way past going to the hospital for chemotherapy. He'd been getting the treatments at home, a nurse coming twice a week, turning home into hospital.

Mel was too weak to walk. I had to get a wheelchair for him. The people in the crowded elevator looked at us with a pity I wanted to throw back into their faces.

On the secretary's desk there was a heart-shaped box of chocolates. A pink ribbon across it spelled out L, O, V, E.

That was the moment when I knew this would be our last trip to that office. And that Mel would hear the words I'd kept from him for nearly twenty-three months.

"It's Valentine's Day," I told him.

He was leaning back with his eyes closed. After a moment, I felt a slight pressure from his fingers, so I knew he'd heard me.

While he was being examined, I sat alone in Dr. Hohlman's office, staring at the mementos on his desk and windowsill that I'd long memorized. There was a new one: a papier-mâché replica of a doctor with a long black cotton beard. Had some patient given him this in the hope of currying a good prognosis in return?

Maybe I should have tried that, I think, staring at a miniature Snow White followed by seven happy-looking dwarves. Would it have changed that scene when I last saw Dr. Hohlman?

It had been in the hospital when Mel was recovering—not recovering—from the tube insertion. I'd been with him all day. Leaving late at night, I stopped in the nurses' station. Dr. Hohlman was there.

"I'm not optimistic," he told me.

I didn't answer.

"Do you understand?" he said.

I leaned against the cool tiles of the wall.

"How long?" I asked.

Dr. Hohlman was coming back with Mel, half carrying him into the room, putting him in the chair beside me. No one spoke. I looked past the defeat on the doctor's face to the corner of the room, where his newest toy sat on the floor, a spiral metal tower with water sliding down it, glistening against the gold-green copper. I concentrated on the drops splashing into the bottom.

". . . isn't making a dent," Dr. Hohlman was saying. "I would be doing you a disservice to continue the treatments."

I waited for Mel to look at me, but his eyes were fixed on Dr. Hohlman. I looked down at Mel's left hand, limp on the arm of the chair. He'd moved his wedding ring to the middle finger, because his ring finger was so thin now the band kept falling off. Did people get buried with their wedding rings? If he didn't want to, what should I do with the ring? Would I wear two?

"How long until I die?" Mel was asking.

"Hard to say."

"A few months?"

Dr. Hohlman's eyes flickered toward me. I knew—he knew—it would be far less than that.

"Probably," he told Mel.

There was silence, broken only by the water falling steadily into that copper base.

"*C'est la vie,*" said Mel.

WHEN WE got home, he collapsed on the stairs in the entryway, unable to climb the three steps into the living room. He hadn't spoken since we'd left the doctor's office.

I sat on the step beside him, my arm around his shoulder, both of us in our bulky winter coats.

"I'm not being Pollyanna," I said, playing the role I'd gotten too used to, "but as the saying goes, 'It ain't over till it's over.' And Hohlman did say you'd probably regain some strength for a while."

He stared down at our hands entwined in his lap.

"You never know what might happen," I struggled on.

"Sssh," he said gently.

I leaned my head against his shoulder. He put his arm around me. The two of us cried together, finally.

Later we sat on the couch and tried to put some words together.

"Sometimes I think I have a kind of death wish," he said. "That's what Ruben told me three years ago, before I got sick. He asked me once if I really wanted to live. I told him I wasn't sure."

"Why not?" I asked, immediately searching through the rubble for what I must have done to make him feel that way.

"That was when I changed jobs. I never felt really comfortable with the new staff. I'd been so close to everyone on the old magazine after twenty years. As if they were my family. But these people seemed so businesslike by comparison. And I think," he said, "maybe I still have a kind of death wish."

"Are you saying that's what you want?"

"I don't know. There's also this wish to live."

"I hope so." I stroked the hand that had the gold band on the wrong finger. "What I think," I said, steering my voice, "is that whatever time we have left, let's do something with it. Know what I mean?" I sound like a grade-B movie, I thought. It seemed safe to try that out on him.

"Do you think we're in a bad movie?"

"No," he said. "It's real."

He tried to smile at me. "I love you," he said.

"I love you, too."

And that's our miracle, I thought. Under all those petty resentments that accumulate in a marriage, we find we still love each other after all. It's so hard to recognize love sometimes, like glimpsing someone on the street and thinking, "Do I know that person? The face looks familiar."

In that moment, the phone rang. It was Norman.

"I have a desire," Mel murmured into the receiver, "to drift off into nothingness. But I feel that I have to be responsible for Anne."

"AND THAT's the moment I'll never get out of my mind," I tell Joseph. "What I did then was so unforgivable."

"What did you do?"

Erupted into a blinding rage. Broke a dish. It crashed into unmendable fragments. Picking them up, I cut my finger.

Mel called to me to hang up the phone for him. I held out my bleeding hand. He stared past it, unseeing.

"Why did you tell Norm that?" I said. "That you have to be 'responsible' for me? That's not what you were saying before. You said you had a death wish."

He was leaning back on the couch, eyes closed.

"Listen to me," I said. "You have no right to say it's because of me."

He waved a tired hand. "All right."

I stared at the closed eyes shutting me out.

"I'm angry."

"Oh, Christ. Come here. Sit next to me." Eyes still closed.

"No!" I ran up the stairs.

In the bathroom, I washed the cut on my finger, wrapped a Band-Aid around it, splashed cold water into my face over and over again. I felt myself turning into stone.

I went downstairs, sat beside him, staring into space, not feeling a goddamn thing.

"AND THEN," I tell Joseph, "I told him . . ." Putting my hands over my face, I sob so violently I almost throw up.

"What?"

"*Everything*. All the things that had been bottled up inside me."

"LET ME tell you about 'responsibility,' " I said. "I knew what Hohlman was going to tell you today, because he told me weeks ago when you were in the hospital. But I kept it from you."

Mel didn't answer. I'll never know what his expression was, because I didn't look at him. I just kept staring straight ahead, feeling the not-feeling.

"I've known from the beginning," I told him, "but I never let you know. I shielded you from phone calls, from messages, from everyone who might upset you. And I did it *alone*, hear me? For most of the time, I had no one in the whole world I felt safe sharing it with. So don't tell me about 'responsible.' "

His hand reached for mine. But I couldn't make myself reach back.

"Thank you," he said.

"For what?" I cried out. "For *what*?"

"For letting me know you're so responsible. It frees me."

To leave me, I thought.

"It's going to be harder for me than for you," I said.

"Yes, it will. What will you do?"

"I've even thought about that. See how 'responsible' I can be? Maybe I'll take our trip to Italy."

"That would be nice."

"Oh, God! How do you expect me to go where we would have been together? Everywhere I turn, I'll be thinking what we would have done together. How am I supposed to enjoy that?"

"It would be good if you could."

I slapped my bandaged hand against the sofa. The not-feeling had ended. It hurt.

"What's the point of all this? What's the point of talking this way?"

"It helps me to know everything you've been feeling."

Not *everything*, I thought. And turned, finally, to look at that poor wasted imitation of his face.

"Don't be angry," he said.

"I'm not. I'm just alone."

"That's true." He closed his eyes again. "You're alone."

"How could I have done that to him?" I ask Joseph.

"But you weren't angry at *him*. You were angry at the situation. Both of you were. And both of you were doing what you had to in order to let go of each other."

Suddenly I'm back in those moments. I see myself kicking and screaming like a child terrified because she's being abandoned. And I realize that what I was angry about was that he *wanted* to die, was willing to *leave* me.

Maybe that was the real start of my widowhood.

I ASKED Mel to write me a letter so I'd have a message from him afterwards.

Too weak to get up from the sofa, he asked me to bring him paper and a pen. I brought him bright blue stationery and left him alone to write. When I came back, he gestured toward the sealed envelope beside him. I took it upstairs and hid it in my bureau drawer.

The next morning he asked me, "Did you read my letter?"

"No," I said, startled. "I told you, it's for . . . later."

That evening he asked, "You haven't read my letter yet?" The writer in him.

So I got the letter and sat beside him reading it. It's a good thing I read it then, because there was one word of his always half-illegible writing that I couldn't make out.

"What's this?" I pointed to the word.

"Afflicted."

I read the rest of the letter.

"Well, thanks," I said.

Couldn't even say what a treasure of a letter. Couldn't even feel anything, except is that *all*? It was such a brief note. Is this all I'm going to have of you through the years ahead?

I guess he knew, because then I leaned my head against his arm and wept.

"It's a beautiful letter," I said. I hope I said.

His letter goes in my suitcase every time I take a trip. I xeroxed two extra copies, put one in the safe deposit box. But I don't have to worry about losing it; I've memorized each word and punctuation mark. Sometimes late at night when I can't sleep, I repeat the words to myself like a mantra.

Sweetheart,

If I should die before you, I would want you to live out your life as fully and joyously as you can.

You have a wonderful capacity for living, and I want you to take every advantage of it.

You also have a superb talent for writing and you must let that flourish.

And, darling, please no guilt about me. If you had been a better wife you would have been close to the angels, and I don't know if I could have been happy with that.

Finally, I cannot know but I can guess how difficult it will be for you to live alone. Darling, I will be as close as God permits, and you must call on all your friends, family and your own resources to get you through it.

Please, darling, don't follow me to the grave. I am afflicted and may have to go, but you are such a wonderful creature of life you belong here.

> With all my deepest love,
> Mel

The envelope was addressed To My Beloved One.

27

THE MONUMENT COMPANY is in a dusty store in a run-down neighborhood on the lower East Side. Four other customers—an elderly man leaning despondently on a cane, and three women wrapped in dark shawls—sit silently in a semicircle near the front of the store. Framed in the dim light filtering through the window, their matching mournful faces look like a scene from a painting.

Mr. Silverstone leads Dorothy and me into the "display" area, a long narrow hallway between brick walls. There's no heat out here and the damp chill freezes our feet. Lined up along the wall are about two dozen tombstones. I never knew they came in so many shapes and sizes, even different colors.

"That one looks like plastic," Dorothy whispers, pointing to a shiny black stone.

Some of the monuments are squared off at the top, others rounded, and one rises in a sloping pyramid with an open book carved on top. Seeing it, I'm tempted, thinking again that Mel deserves the "best"—whatever that is. This is how costs get

150

jacked up. He used to get so frustrated by my weakness with salespeople, when I'd agree with them that we "must have" all those extras. Like the dishwasher model I insisted on buying because of the "Extra Cleaning" and "Hold" cycles that we've never used in ten years.

A lot of the stones have flowers etched into them. One gray stone has a small oval frame set in the middle. From within it, the pastel face of a young woman with sorrowful eyes stares back at us.

"Always Remembered," swear a lot of the stones, but the favorite slogan seems to be *"Forever In Our Hearts."*

Forever. Always. How hopeful.

We notice that some of the stones just have the birth date, not the year when the person died. When we ask him about this, Mr. Silverstone clears his throat delicately. He then informs us that a lot of people order their own stones "ahead of time" to save the family the "bother."

It makes me feel remiss. What would I put on mine: *She Couldn't Decide?*

I sit on an uncomfortable concrete bench staring at the array of tombstones. What decorations would I like, Mr. Silverstone wants to know. My mind goes blank. Minutes pass. Dorothy loyally shivers beside me. Mr. Silverstone reminds us that it's cold out here. Is it my fault he doesn't have his trophies in a warmer setting? I think enviously of a friend who scattered her husband's ashes from a plane, across the mountains he had loved. Of course, that meant going up in a plane! But at least she didn't have to sit in this macabre place, making these impossible decisions.

Finally, I opt for simplicity. The only decoration I want is a Star of David. But Mr. Silverstone, a diligent salesman, points to a carving of the eternal flame. It reminds me of President Kennedy. Yes, my husband would like that, I tell him.

"Do you prefer to have it set in a square or a circle?" Mr. Silverstone asks, pointing to examples of each style. But I've used up my decision-making capability. Dorothy comes to my rescue by reminding me that a circle is a symbol of eternity.

How about the border? There's one that curves, another in loops. No, I tell him, I want a plain one. "Line rule," I say, dredging the term up from my editing years, trying to sound professional. Or at least sane.

Mr. Silverstone hurries us to the warmth inside so I can "place an order."

He asks for the dates of birth and death, and Mel's father's name.

"I want his mother's included, too," I say.

"That's not the customary procedure."

"I don't care, I want it. My husband was very close to his mother." She's right across the path now.

I write out the inscription on a small memo pad he pushes toward me:

BELOVED HUSBAND
FATHER, POET

Then I ask if there will be room for four more words. I didn't clear those with Mel, but it's my choice now, isn't it?

What I want added at the bottom—"in script," I tell him (how calm she is, how controlled)—is:

Good Night, Sweet Prince

Mr. Silverstone whips out an oversized slide rule, meticulously measures.

"It will fit," he says. "And no extra charge."

28

Is it possible that I've lived without him for a whole year?

The day we all dread the most is the anniversary of the death. A booklet warns that around this time we may feel "incapacitated." That's certainly the word for it! All February I've been unable to focus on anything else, as though I'm hearing the world from under water. I'm all the way back to zero.

"Make plans for the day," advise the group veterans. "Don't be alone."

"You'll feel better if you go to the cemetery," says a man who "visits" his wife every Sunday.

Mel didn't believe in visiting cemeteries. I'll feel closer to him if I go to a place he loved, the Metropolitan Museum of Art. It's the first time I'm not avoiding a scene that holds memories. Maybe that's progress, but on this day I don't care. It's the past I crave, not the future.

Dorothy—who's certainly earned the Friendship Medal this year—offers to go with me. "Want to see the new Fauve exhibit?" she asks, anxious to do right by this day.

Yes. Why not? Anything.

But surrounded by brilliant colors on every wall, all I can see is the grayness of the hospice, the grayness of his face. At 3:35 P.M. I back into a corner, pretending to be absorbed by the painting in front of me.

"Peace," I whisper to him, "for *both* of us."

HE WANTED to die at home, but he never asked how I felt about that. It was Dr. Hohlman who asked me, "Do you think you can handle it?"

"I don't know," I said.

Dr. Hohlman looked at me with such concern, I wanted to lean my head against his chest and cry.

"We're going to get you some help," he said.

Someone was supposed to contact us about setting up a hospice at home, but days passed and no one called. Mel faded, not eating, barely drinking water. He was in bed all the time, except when he had to get up to go to the bathroom. He was supposed to wake me up to help him, but twice he didn't— and fell, crashing to the floor. I leaped out of bed screaming, fumbling for the silent figure on the floor in the darkness, not knowing if he was still alive. Miraculously, he wasn't hurt.

Frantic, I called Dr. Hohlman, who was surprised no one had shown up. "I'll see what I can do," he said. (Doctor, you're supposed to be powerful, don't let me know now that you're not.)

A nurse finally arrived to see what kind of help we needed. She confided to me that Mel looked "a lot better" than she'd expected. "If you can get him to eat, he'll probably last for another year."

Where do they find people who tell you fairy tales like that? Deliver me from them, give me the rough movie-character type who barks, "I'll give it to you straight." He had six days left.

"She says if you'll eat you'll live for another year," I told him. "And by then they may have found a new treatment . . ."

"Why don't you just let me go?" he said wearily. "How can you even want me the way I am now?"

Because I can't imagine a life or world without you, I thought. Sitting on the edge of the bed, I put my arm around that pitifully bony shoulder.

"Oh, God," he said, "if I could only die in this moment with your arm around me like this."

"My arms will be around you," I promised.

The nurse had asked Mel if he'd like oxygen to help him breathe more easily. But he didn't want anything that reminded him of a hospital. She assured him it would just be an "unobtrusive" plastic tube that he could place under his nose. A few hours later, equipment was delivered: two large canisters on wheels. Plus a portable commode. He was distraught when those things were wheeled in. And I was terrified when the man delivering them tried to show me how to operate the oxygen. If I pushed the wrong lever, would Mel suffocate?

"I told you I didn't want anything like this," Mel said, angry at me for turning the room into a hospital. But *you're* the one who wanted to die at home, I thought. And you never asked how I felt about that responsibility. I had nightmares about him dying in the middle of the night; he was threatening to take an overdose of something.

I stroked his hand, trying to calm him.

"Please have a Sustacal."

"I'll try," he said.

Just then the phone rang. Always that phone at the wrong time. This call was from an editor I was working for. I talked to her for maybe five minutes, but it was long enough for Mel to change his mind.

"Chocolate or vanilla?" I asked.

"Nothing," he mumbled, eyes closed again.

"You said you'd have one."

"Don't ask me anymore."

"There's no point in my being here if you won't listen to me," I said. "I'll leave and let someone else take my place." He didn't answer. I stormed downstairs, made hot tea, sat there trying to get hold of myself. I came back upstairs and stood in the doorway looking at him.

"Kill me," he said, "but don't get angry at me."

We had fought on what turned out to be his last night at home.

I had to go to the airport to pick up David, who was coming for the weekend. It's only a ten-minute drive, but I was torn between anxiety at leaving Mel alone and a suffocating need to get out of the apartment for a while.

"You're sure you'll be okay?" I asked him.

"I'll be okay."

"Promise you won't get out of bed?"

"Don't worry."

I put the phone on the bed beside him and raced to the airport. David's plane was delayed. I wanted to call Mel, but there were long lines in front of all the phones. Running down the hallways, I grabbed one that was free. It rang six times before he picked it up.

"You woke me," he said sleepily.

"I just wanted to make sure you're okay. I'm sorry for what happened before."

"What happened?"

It's like Joseph keeps saying, the guilt I'm carrying around isn't between Mel and me, but between me and me.

But the guiltiest refrain that keeps echoing in the group is, "I wasn't with him at the end." Haunted voices recounting what can never be undone: *They had sent me home*" ; "*The doctor said I should get some sleep*" ; "*I'd left for just ten minutes to get coffee . . .*"

How easily Mel might have died while I was at the airport, because David's plane ended up being two hours late. We might have come home to find Mel dead. I would have agonized for the rest of my life about whether he had been calling for me, how had he felt, had he known, was he frightened?

But God allowed us to be together.

During the night, Mel started throwing up green watery bile. In the morning, I had to make a decision.

"I know I promised you could be home," I told him, while an ashen-faced David stood in the doorway listening. "But the hospice can take better care of you than I can. And the nurse said it's a private section, not like a hospital. I'll be able to sleep in the room with you. Is that all right?"

He reached for my hand. "You'll stay with me?"

"I won't leave you for a minute."

So he agreed. But I had to be sure he understood what we were really doing.

"You realize this means you may not come home?"

"I know."

A HOSPICE is a place where—if you have to die—it's a good place to do it. The whole process of dying is respected, the way birth is in a happier ward. Everything possible is done to help the person have a "good" death.

Mel was put in a large room that looked more like an old-fashioned hotel than a hospital, with pink walls and a high ceiling. There was one other patient on the other side of the curtain: a man with a brain tumor. His teenage son was visiting him before leaving for college. The wife had died just months before. The boy stood there, turning his baseball cap around and around in his hands, telling his father what courses he'd signed up for. His father couldn't understand.

A nurse gave Mel an injection that not only calmed him, it sent him into a state of euphoria. The children sat by his bed (Tamar had come racing there), and Mel talked frenetically, exuberantly.

Turning to me, he said, "I want you to marry again."

"Sure," I said.

Moments later, he asked, "Are you going to sit *shivah* for me?"

"All seven days," I told him.

"Oh, shit! Three is enough."

The children laughed, looking at him adoringly. He grinned, delighted with himself.

"I hope the weather's good for the funeral," he said. "I don't want people to have to stand in the rain." I thought we must have been transported to an insane asylum.

Suddenly two figures appeared in the room: it was a moment before I recognized Lee and Stan. Someone—was it me?—must have called them.

"Stan," Mel asked, "if I get out of this place alive, may I borrow your copy of *The Decline and Fall of the Roman Empire?*"

"You sure can," Stan said.

The children went home to get some sleep. I lay on a cot alongside Mel's bed, holding his hand through the railing. On the other side of the curtain, the man with the brain tumor kept calling out incomprehensible syllables. Several times I stumbled sleepily over to ask what he wanted. He stared at me with terrified eyes, pointing to the floor, the wall, the ceiling. Finally I went down the deserted hallway in search of help.

I asked if Mel could be moved to a private room. The nurse said those were reserved for "serious" cases.

The next morning the hospice physician told me Mel seemed better. "I wouldn't be surprised if he's able to go home and be all right for a few more weeks."

("Dr. Optimist," Tamar called him bitterly.)

Mel's euphoria of the night before had worn off. He didn't remember that incredible scene, but Tamar and David will never forget that evening of antic laughter. It was their father's final gift to them.

The day passed slowly. The children came and went, going out for meals. I stayed in Mel's room. Someone brought me trays of food, but for the first time in my life I couldn't eat.

Saturday night Mel was restless, loud whooshing sounds when he breathed, as though his lungs were filling up with water. Toward dawn, I gave up trying to sleep and sat on the edge of his bed.

"Did you get any sleep?" I asked him.

"Not really. Did you?"

"Not really."

"That's togetherness." It was the last coherent sentence he ever said to me.

He dozed off. I tried to edit an article that was due the next day. Suddenly I became aware that his breathing had changed, become more labored. I rushed to get a nurse.

"The dying has begun," she said.

So then he merited a private room. "The family can have privacy that way," the nurse said.

That night the children slept on couches in the lounge. I lay awake on the cot beside Mel's bed, holding his hand through the bars as he slept. The door opened quietly and a nun stood there, almost as broad as the doorway. She gestured me into the hall.

"I'm Sister Mary Loyola. I have something that your son thought you might need. He said you could use a little cheering up." And from a hidden pocket in her massive smock she pulled out a bottle of wine!

I laughed. "I don't think I'm up to that."

"You need something to warm you during all of this," she insisted, leading me down the hall to the lounge. There were my children, guzzling her wine.

"Perhaps this would be better?" asked Sister.

And from another pocket came a bottle of bourbon.

I was afraid to leave his room, terrified he might die in that second when my back was turned. I left only to go to the bathroom, dashing down the hall and back. Twice I ran to the nurses' bath to take a one-minute shower, racing back down the corridor in my robe, soaking wet.

Monday morning, David said we should call Mel's publisher, Chuck Wrye.

"He didn't know Daddy was this sick; he'll be angry we didn't tell him," I said (worried about Mel's job!).

"Ma, what difference does it make?"

Ten minutes after David called him, Chuck was at the hospice to say good-bye to Mel.

"The magazine has had its best year ever," Chuck told him. "There's a bonus waiting for you. We'll make sure that Anne gets it." Some sound like a pleased "oh" came from Mel.

Then, without my knowing it, Chuck called everyone who had ever worked with Mel. All that day—and the next—they kept arriving: his current staff, and all the ones from his former magazine whom he'd liked to call "my people."

Gladys and Norm flew in. Herb came.

"May I have a few minutes alone with Mel?" Herb asked.

"I'll be right outside the door," I said reluctantly.

I didn't know until later that Herb wanted to tell Mel he "forgave" him for hurts all those years. I wish Mel had been able to answer, "I forgive you, too, brother!"

Then, in an incredible parade, friends began arriving, having apparently set up a relay on the phone. Dorothy, Charlie, Blanche, Edie and Chuck, Yvonne, our old college trio, people we hadn't seen for years, traveling hours to spend two minutes by Mel's bedside to say good-bye.

That night, I let down the bars on the side of the bed, climbed in with Mel, and lay there with my arms around him. Tamar opened the door and saw us there.

"Please stay like that with Daddy," she said.

So that's how everyone saw us the next day, both of us in that narrow bed. I half sat up, trying to greet them, pointing out each one to Mel, who'd wave a fragile greeting, dazed from the morphine given to him to allay anxiety.

But it upset him to be so confused. So I asked the nurse to hold off on the morphine the next day (by the grace of God he had no pain). I knew it upset him, even then, to look unkempt in front of his staff, so I asked the nurse to give him a shave and dress him in clean new pajamas instead of that hospital robe. He looked almost like himself again, propped up against pillows, smiling at the friends and staffers who crowded around trying to smile back at him.

In the midst of this bizarre farewell party, the phone rang. It was Ruben, wanting to say something to Mel. I put the receiver against his ear. Ruben told him, "It's all right to let go now."

Mel's eyes rolled up toward the ceiling. I thought he was going to die within seconds.

"Get out!" I screamed at all those visitors.

Holding Mel, I kept saying, "My love goes with you, your love stays with me . . . my love . . . your love . .," over and over again.

"I let you go," I told him. But he clung to life.

Hours passed. The children kept coming in and out.

"Has everyone left?" I asked.

"Are you kidding?" said Tamar. "*No* one's leaving!"

They all stayed to the very end, taking over the entire lounge in an all-night vigil.

Alone with Mel, I asked God for one last favor. "Please let him open his eyes and look at me once more. Let us have a few more words together. Please, let him know me."

Mel opened his eyes. Not dazed. Knowing me.

"Everyone's staying," I told him. "See how much they care about you?"

"Nice," he whispered.

"I love you," I told him.

". . . love you . . ."

Reaching up, he stroked my cheek.

"Kiss me," I begged. Leaning down, I brought my face close to his. His lips moved against my cheek.

WEDNESDAY MORNING, the nurse said the room should be quiet so he could "leave peacefully." At intervals someone would tiptoe in, ask in a whisper if I needed anything, was there anything I wanted? I shook my head. What I "needed," what I "wanted," was slipping away from me.

I lay there holding Mel, my arm cramped. Sometimes I'd sit up on the edge of the bed, trying to stretch my back. But I always tried to keep a smile of sorts, so he wouldn't think I was trying to stop him from leaving.

Around noon, the children and I were alone in the room with him. Tamar was sitting by the other side of the bed, her face buried in the blanket. David was dozing in a chair in the corner.

And suddenly, I saw . . . something . . . Some kind of pale yellow light shaped like a figure, slowly sitting up out of Mel's body and soundlessly rising away from it . . .

Then I felt something, someone, standing behind me, watching all of us. Without turning around, I lifted my hand to my shoulder and reached back, so that spirit, light—whatever, whomever—would know I understood.

MORE TIME went by. The children had left the room, unable to bear any more. Norman opened the door. I gestured to him to come in.

Silently, he stood by the head of the bed, stroking his brother's forehead. I kept my arm around Mel, so it would be there in that moment we were waiting for.

"My love goes with you, your love stays with me," I whispered over and over again.

His breaths became slower and softer, more spaced out. Norman and I would wait, holding our own breath, to see if there would be another one. The intervals got longer.

"Is he . . . ?" I started to whisper at one point.

No, there was still another gentle breath, in, out . . .

Seconds passed, but this time there was no breath in.

And so, at 3:35 P.M., he died.

In my arms. As promised.

29

"I was there for you, why the hell aren't you here for me?"

That's what a woman in the group confesses yelling at her husband's picture when she was facing a scary biopsy.

What hangs over all of us is the spectre of being ill, alone. Julie has the flu. Afterwards, she tells me, "It really brings it home to you how alone you are. I didn't even have enough food in the house."

"Next time," I advise, with more assuredness than I feel, "get the phone numbers of take-out places, so you can call for meals. And drugstores, so they can deliver medicine."

"I never thought of that," she says.

We're all so reluctant to face the fact that we have to take care of ourselves now. My terror is of having a heart attack during the night. Dying alone. Not surrounded by love, the way he was. Incredibly, I'm jealous of that!

My stomach feels tense, maybe it's *my* turn to have cancer. That's how his started. Everyone in the group is having symptoms. "Thinking you have the same ones keeps you connected, too," Nedda says.

I have to have gum surgery. I come home in pain, frightened. How am I going to manage? I lie in bed bathed in self-pity. I'm supposed to take an antibiotic and a painkiller, but I left them downstairs, don't have the energy to go down to get them. If Mel were here, he'd get them for me. Bring me hot tea with honey in it.

"Damn it!" I say to no one. I get up, dizzy. If I fall down the stairs, how long would I lie there before someone discovered the body? I make it safely down the stairs and back into bed. I feel an odd kind of triumph.

Joseph warns me that grief weakens your immune system, so I better start eating decent meals. When Mel was ill, I used to lecture him about eating more nutritiously. "Will you at least try to have eggs? They're easy to get down." He said, "I'm worried about cholesterol."

"You took care of Mel," says Joseph. "Now you have to take care of Anne." I dimly remember some woman who was able to take care of her dying husband, make decisions for him, keep his morale up. How come she has so little strength for herself?

Obediently I go to a produce store, stare at broccoli, lettuce, cantaloupes as though they're foreign items. Buy them, hoping they won't rot in the refrigerator.

MAYBE IT'S my *mind* that's ill. There are so many things I can't do. Still haven't been keeping track of expenses, don't know how much money I have, what interest is coming in from CD's and other things, forgot to file quarterly taxes, which I should be doing as a free-lancer.

Doing an errand for a neighbor, I come out to my car to find a ticket on the windshield. Apparently I've been driving all year with an expired inspection sticker. (I seem to have misplaced a whole year!) I'm furious that I got a ticket when I was doing a good deed for someone. "Give me a break," I tell God.

I'm angry so much of the time. At the mailman for leaving a package outside the screen door where prowlers will notice that no one's home, at Herb and Vella for continuing to ignore me, at everyone who wasn't "there" for us when Mel was ill.

"I'll never forgive anyone who hurt Mel," I tell Ruben.

"What you're really in a rage about," he says, "is being left alone. All the rest is commentary."

In the middle of the night I wake up knowing what's beneath that, too. What I'm really angry about, down into my bones, is that I feel no one cares about me anymore. The top third of my head tells me this isn't true—children, friends—but even louder than the widow in me, the infant in me cries, UNLOVED. And every trivial thing calls that up. The oven breaks down. Sears promises to replace the part within a few days. A week later, I call to ask where it is.

"We can't give you an exact date," says the bored voice at the other end of the wire.

"But I can't use my stove, the gas has been turned off."

"Maybe by the end of the month."

"I can't cook anything," I scream. "And I'm alone here." I slam the phone down, sobbing hysterically. Sears doesn't love me, either.

Getting into bed, I whimper into Mel's pillow that I can't go on, *won't* go on. I fantasize turning on the gas, sticking my head in the oven, the note on the dining table telling my children, "Sorry." But a part of me laughs at myself. Suicide in the *oven*? It isn't even working!

A friend invites me to a charades party. A party? That belongs to a time when the biggest problem was what to wear. "I'm not up to a party," I tell her. Especially not charades. We used to play years ago, with our actor friends. Mel, inhibited in so many other ways, unabashedly contorting his long body into pretzel poses, gesturing furiously when his team (particularly me!) didn't guess fast enough.

I challenge myself to go to the party.

"You're great at charades," my teammates tell me. The actress in me feels alive. Sitting down flushed with pride at the applause after my turn, I look out the window wondering if he's watching.

One of the women tells me she was widowed five years ago, why don't we meet for dinner sometime and "cry together"? She smiles as she says it, mocking the words.

Over a dinner I can't afford, she tells me that happiness does eventually come back into your life. "Of course," she says, "my lover has made all the difference."

I keep the smile pasted on my face, in another kind of charade. She goes home to someone. He's glad to see her, puts his arms around her, asks her how she is.

"Wouldn't you like to find someone?" she asks me.

Looking away, I see my face in the mirror on the wall opposite. The tense lines, grayer hair. But the face one man loyally thought "beautiful" doesn't look *too* old. Yet.

"I don't know," I answer. "Maybe. I guess so."

By her third drink, this woman's confessing, "I've never felt really great since my husband died." The liveliness drains from her eyes. "It never completely goes away," she says.

Afterwards, waiting in an icy drizzle for my express bus, I long to get on one of the local buses instead, riding back and forth across the city all night, just to be with other bodies.

Home, I stare at Mel's picture. Suddenly my hand moves in a swift gesture, as though slapping him across the face.

"Why did you leave me?" I scream at him.

I USED to have music on all the time, but now the stereo and CD player are dusty. I turn on the CD, but the drawer won't open. Panic time. (Every time something goes wrong in the apartment I feel less in control of my life.) How do I disconnect all these wires to get it to a repair store? And how do I find one that won't cheat me? Trying to get the drawer open, I give it a gingerly tug. You're going to break it, I warn myself, but I suddenly need to feel I'm capable of taking care of things. I push it in, then try to edge it out again. The drawer slides open!

I go to the florist to buy a bouquet for a friend. "Will that be all?" asks the clerk. Through the chilled plate glass, I stare at the purple and yellow irises. Mel used to bring home flowers every Friday night. I hear myself saying, "I'll take another bunch—for me."

I tackle another free-lance assignment, for that editor who said my writing had lost its "bounciness." After I send in the article, he phones. "You're back to your old style!"

I report my progress to the group.

Helen, a newcomer, shakes her head. "The problem is, we just inch forward in millimeters."

"Yes," I tell her, "but it's the millimeters that we have to be aware of."

I HAVE a very different kind of dream. About *Tom Sawyer*, of all things. The part where he and Becky are lost in the cave, with only one candle left. Tom says they have to try to find a way out, but Becky's exhausted and hopeless. She tells him to go on without her and leave her to die. Promising to return soon, he takes a ball of twine to unravel as he goes, so he can find his way back to her. Holding the sole candle, he stumbles along the winding corridors of the cave until the twine runs out. He's about to turn back, when suddenly the candle blows out.

But in my dream I call to him, "Tom, can you hear me? If the candle went out it must have been from a gust of air. And if air, then a way *out*."

And the Tom in my dream hears me, feels his way farther along the damp, dark sides of the cave.

"Look, Tom," I call, "look up!"

And there it is—a faint patch of light way above. A way out.

And what does Tom do—in the book, in my dream? He gropes his way back to Becky to lead her out, too.

I tell Joseph about my dream.

"Do you see what it means?" he asks.

"I guess I'm Becky, alone in the darkness."

"But you also identified with Tom, who found the way out. So what does that mean to you?"

I stare across the small room. "That I'm trying to rescue myself, to lead *me* out of the tunnel?"

He nods.

I feel as if I've reached some kind of turning point.

30

I'M HAVING LUNCH with Kitty, from the support group. She's always struck me as rather timid, but today she gives me a defiant look.

"See this?" she asks, holding out her left hand. "I took off my ring."

I stare at the bare finger. "How does it feel?"

"As if I'm a different person. A single woman."

"You don't want to wear it on your right hand?"

"No. But I know someone who wears her ring on a chain around her neck."

I feel strangled at the thought.

"I put mine in my bureau drawer," she says. "Do you think it matters?"

"You inspire me," I tell her.

Riding home on the bus that night, I look at my reflection in the window and see a hand resting on my arm. For a moment, I think it's Mel's hand. Then I recognize my own. The light of a passing car shines on my gold band. I put a finger across it, hiding it, trying to imagine my hand without it.

Mel is still wearing his ring. That's one decision I didn't have trouble making. We have matching bands. I remember the day we bought them, in my uncle's jewelry company because he'd said he'd give us a discount. But he wasn't very happy when we told him what inscriptions we wanted: not just our initials and the date, but quotations. "The lettering is going to cost more than the rings," my uncle said. But we insisted.

"All For Love," mine reads.

When the men came to remove Mel from the hospice, I asked them to be careful not to lose the ring, because it was so loose on his finger. They told me to take it and put it on him in the funeral parlor. For the two days before, I was anxiety-ridden about whether I'd be able to get it on him. Did fingers get rigid? Would the people in charge forget and lock the coffin?

I wanted to give him something else, too: a copy of his poems, which he'd had privately printed years ago. It's titled, LIMITS.

"The coffin's closed," I cried out, when I walked into the chapel early. "They promised I could see him."

"No problem," said an attendant, sliding the top off. I never knew the lids go on and off so easily.

"How efficient," I said.

And there he was, dressed in his yarmulke and tallis, the way he was on religious holidays. I touched his face. "How cold he is," I said. As though he'd just come in from shoveling snow.

Carefully I straightened his finger; it moved easily. I slipped the ring on, remembering when we'd first put the rings on each other's fingers. "My love goes with you," I told him for the last time. "Your love stays with me." I placed the copy of his poems under his folded hands. Leaning over, I kissed his forehead.

"Sleep well," I told him.

"WHAT A lovely funeral." I never understood that cliché before. Mel's was a real hit, as they say in the theatre. More than three hundred people showed up, flying in from all over the country because he was so well-known in the travel industry. We had to be moved to the largest chapel.

But it all felt like a play. Even the black dress I'd borrowed from Edie seemed like a costume. When I was getting dressed, my sister had objected to my not wearing make-up. (You're not supposed to, according to ritual, and I was big on ritual that day.) "Mel wouldn't want you to look like this," Sonia said. So I sneaked on some base to hide the tense lines in my face. No lipstick because red is too joyous and no mascara because it would get messy if I cried.

But I was determined *not* to cry. Isn't that the criterion for widows—how well they "hold up" at the funeral? "She didn't shed one tear." The ultimate in praise, the Jackie Kennedy role. And I wanted my children to be proud of me.

David had cued me by telling me how "wonderful" his friend's mother had been at her husband's funeral. "She was great all those months afterwards, too," he said (translated into, didn't make problems for *her* son). He failed to mention that later this stoical woman had a stroke.

When David arrived at the chapel, he was carrying a small brown grocery bag. In it was a corned-beef sandwich on rye bread, complete with pickles, from a deli he and Mel used to eat in. Then David sat on the carpet alongside the coffin and proceeded to eat his sandwich!

"You can't do that here," I whispered, shocked.

"It's my last lunch with Daddy."

People began arriving. I heard a voice that was probably mine reciting, "How nice of you to come" . . . "Of course, I remember you . . ." From some kind of distance, I was surprised at how solemn everyone looked.

We were led into the chapel. Breaking away from the attendant escorting us, I put my hand on top of the closed coffin. "I'm here," I told Mel, the way I had all those months.

But that final gesture felt like acting, too, because I was watching myself doing it.

* * *

"I'LL TELL you what I'd like at my funeral," Mel said. It was the day after Dr. Hohlman had told him the truth.

I got a legal pad and pen, dutifully making notes. As though we were planning one of the New Year's Eve parties we used to give so successfully.

"There are some lines from a poem of Whitman's that I'd like to have read," he said. "But it has to be by someone who can read with feeling." Now we were casting a play!

It reminded me of when we were drama counselors at a children's camp, that summer when we were dating. Our big production at the end of the summer was *Where's Charley?* It went over big, and the next morning Mel and I were triumphantly strolling down the country road bordering the camp. I was trying to figure out how to hint that I'd changed my mind after turning down his numerous proposals. I thought I'd marry him after all, but I was too shy to tell him. Instead I started humming one of the songs from the show: *"Make a miracle . . . marry me."*

Oblivious, Mel went on talking about how well the performance had gone.

"Don't you recognize that?" I asked.

"Recognize what?"

"The lines that go with the song I'm humming."

"Did I ever hear it before?"

I'd forgotten he was tone-deaf.

So I had to sing the words—"Make a miracle, marry me"— as we stood there on that dusty road.

"It's a nice song," he said, starting to walk on.

"Mel," I screeched, "I'm saying yes!"

"THE STANZAS I want read," he said, start with *"Come lovely and soothing death . . ."*

I moved my hand back and forth over the notepad, unable to answer.

"How about Lee reading it?" I asked, when I got my voice back.

"She's too controlled."

"Give her a chance," I said, writing "Lee" on the pad.

"The children will want to speak, too," I told him.

"Think so?" he asked, surprised.

"Tamar, David," I wrote. "Your brothers?"

He shrugged. "I doubt that they'll want to." (He was half right; Herb declined.)

"We should have someone from the magazine," I said. "How about Chuck?"

"It wouldn't be appropriate." The eternal editor.

But when Mel couldn't overrule me anymore, I did ask Chuck to speak. "I'm honored," he said, hugging me tearfully in the hallway of the hospice.

Mel would have been pleased with his funeral. *Was* pleased. I know, because I felt him standing near us, a little to the right of the podium.

But most of the funeral seems blurry, like reflections under water.

I remember David MC'd the services, so poised that I knew Mel must be looking at him proudly. Can you believe that's our son? I asked Mel. We were the only ones who'd remember what a shy little boy David had been. Then I realized that the congregation was laughing as David said, "When my mother told my father she was going to sit *shivah* all week, he said, 'Oh, shit! Three days is enough.' " I saw the rabbi trying to control his face and David grinning.

But in a second it all changed, and David was telling everybody how "accepting" Mel had been during that last week, and reciting one of his father's poems:

Not summer is the season I would praise
But early autumn when the cool is come,
That time that faces death without withdrawal . . .

Then Tamar was telling of a time when she was a child at the beach, and had climbed on an empty lifeguard's chair and been afraid to come down. How Mel had encouraged her to overcome her fear. "I'm glad I did. Jump, I mean," she said, brushing tears from her cheeks with the back of her hands, the way she used to when she was a little girl. "My father also taught me that love means letting go."

You taught *me* that, too, those last weeks, I told him.

Then Norman—his voice husky—was telling his brother, "I hardly knew you. Mel, you left too soon."

I remember Lee, the "controlled" one, reading so movingly after apologizing because "it's hard to read with tears in your eyes"; and that Chuck gave a tribute to Mel's status in the travel magazine field and everyone was very impressed; and that a friend of David's read another of Mel's poems . . . But I was in and out of all this, hearing, not hearing, staring at the place where I kept seeing Mel.

The rabbi started intoning a passage he didn't even know was Mel's favorite: *"A time to live, a time to die . . ."*

And that's when I lost it, all that dignified, dry-eyed rot. But silently, because one isn't supposed to break down.

Why the hell not?

Even in that black limousine, riding with David, and Mel's brothers and their wives, all of us laughing hysterically, as we nibbled on cookies and sandwiches we'd sneaked into our pockets. Did the driver think we'd all gone mad—or was he used to temporary insanity?

MONTHS LATER I went to another funeral. The woman's husband was weeping openly, unashamed. I had a fierce longing to recreate that day of Mel's funeral, to sob and scream in front of everyone. As though only that could do justice to him. Why did I think I had to be so damn well-behaved?

Even at the cemetery. Still dry-eyed. But not distant anymore, as they lowered the coffin into that opening in the ground.

"Gently," I told the men, "gently."

In the Jewish tradition, the first dirt is cast by hands that loved the person. My fingers closed around some cold earth. Slowly I moved my hand in small circles, so the soil would fall evenly over the coffin. One by one, the children, his brothers, our friends, threw in more dirt until—so quickly—the coffin was hidden from our sight.

We waited while the gravediggers filled in the rest, patting the dark earth with the backs of their shovels.

Still I stood there, unable to leave him.

"It isn't proper to linger," said the rabbi.

I'VE BEEN lingering ever since, I think, turning the ring around and around in the reflection in the window.

31

Madge calls. She's starting to give away Jack's things!

"If I can give them away," she says, "maybe I can release *myself*." Madge, of all people.

For months I've been telling a woman who cleans apartments for a living that "one of these days" she can have Mel's bed for her son. Getting rid of it will give me more space in the room, but I haven't been able to do it. His bed sits beside mine, useless. That boy needs a decent bed.

After Madge's call, I phone the woman. "Your son can have the bed."

"Are you sure, dear?"

"No," I tell her. "But I never will be. So let him come for it now."

I'd sell Mel's bike if I could get the padlock off. I pull at it in frustration. To my amazement, it opens. All these months, it wasn't even locked. I place an ad in our local newsletter: "BIKE BARGAIN"—barely used, real cheap. (I try to sell his gold-plated chess set, too, but nobody responds to that ad. Bicycling must be more popular than chess; there are a dozen calls about the bike.) The first man who comes to look at it buys instantly. "Enjoy it," I say, caressing the handlebars.

It's only a bicycle, I tell myself.

When I tell Joseph, he gives me his new cheerleader refrain: "I hear progress."

Joseph's getting stricter with me. "Up to now," he says, "your time has been structured by grief. But now you need to fill your life in other ways, so it's less focused on loss." He tells me a lot of widows make plans to take classes, go on trips.

"What can you do *now*?" he asks.

"I don't know." The future seems like a postscript to the past.

"One thing you can do," he says, "is try to make the apartment more *your* experience."

My answer surprises me. "I'll have it painted. Then I'll be able to entertain again."

"I hear progress," he says.

THE APARTMENT looks the way I feel, gray. The walls are supposed to be white, but it's been seven years since they were painted. The plaster's peeling; there are telltale holes where shelves and a hanging lamp used to be.

I'm entitled to a free painting under the terms of the lease. (Did Mel guess why I insisted both our names be on it when we renewed last year?) The landlord's painters have a reputation for "sloshing" on cheap paint, but I don't want to spend money for my own painters. I decide to compromise by buying my own paint. But I forget to do it.

A cabinet has to be taken down in the bathroom. I've never done anything like this. I dig out Mel's dusty toolbox, find three screwdrivers. "One of them has to be a Phillips," I mutter, not knowing what it looks like but remembering that's what Mel said he used. How come none of the widows I know were smart enough to learn how to do these things when our husbands were alive; did we think we'd have that built-in help forever?

The screws are so encrusted with old paint they're almost impossible to turn. Biting down on my lip so hard I taste blood, I wrestle with the first one. It finally turns. I tackle the other three, trying to see through the sweat trickling into my eyes. But I do it, the cabinet comes down!

Emptying the closets, I find Mel's brown tweed L.L. Bean hat. He wore it to hide the baldness from the chemotherapy. I hold it in my hands, unable to throw it away.

Thursday night I look at empty shelves, floors bare of carpets, walls stripped of paintings. There's an echo from my voice when I speak, an echo from my footsteps.

The painter arrives in the morning. He barely speaks English; I don't know a word of Greek. I ask him what his name is. It's hard to decipher the syllables, but I finally realize he's saying, "Ari-stotle." That's not as promising as it sounds.

"These three closets," I say, opening the doors to show him they've been emptied.

He shakes his head. "No closets."

"Since *when*?" My tone is no-nonsense.

"Okay, okay."

"And these shelves." I point to the built-in bookcase.

"No do."

"Why not?"

"Okay, okay."

Scowling, he gestures at the furniture I've pulled into the middle of the bedroom. "How I paint?"

"What am I supposed to do, carry the bureaus downstairs on my back?"

"Okay, okay." He lights a cigarette, throws the match on the floor. I look at the flammable paint in horror. Besides, I'm allergic to cigarette smoke.

"Must you?" I ask, afraid to say don't. He pretends not to understand.

By four o'clock when he leaves, the air is thick with cigarette smoke and dust. The floor's littered with plaster, chips, cigarette butts, smears of paint. What use were those filthy tarpulins he's stored in the corner? (He's coming back Monday to paint the downstairs.)

I go upstairs to cheer myself with my clean white walls. They still look gray! The paint is such a poor grade it didn't even change the hue. I forgot that I was going to buy my own paint. Where's my head these days?

I need to rest, but I can't get into either of the bedrooms. I go down to the living room, but the sofa and chairs are piled with a mountain of things. I spread my coat on the floor and curl up on it sobbing. I feel betrayed by the painting; wasn't it supposed to be "progress"? The phone rings. Racing for it, I fall over a carton.

"I know it's ridiculous to cry about something like this," I tell Dorothy, when I finally reach the phone, "but I can't stand the chaos."

"Maybe it's a metaphor for your whole life."

I spend the weekend carrying everything upstairs because I don't trust Aristotle not to get paint on them. Hundreds of books. The glass top from the coffee table. The sofa cushions. "You're crazy," I hear Mel saying.

But I don't know how to disconnect the TV or stereo. And the dining area buffet is too heavy to budge. How am I supposed to handle all this alone? Why didn't Joseph stop me from this insane project, isn't he supposed to be looking after me? Where the hell is Mel? The children? *Someone.*

I run across the courtyard to a friend of David's. "I've got to have help," I tell Manny incoherently, as he and his brother stare at me. "No problem," they say. Coming back with me, they take care of the stereo, the TV, the buffet.

Manny runs his finger over a bedroom wall. "That's sure a thin paint that guy is using," he says.

All this mess for a third-rate job?

Monday morning Aristotle comes back. Marching him upstairs, I point a stern finger to show him the holes he didn't plaster, the spots he missed.

"While you take care of these," I tell him, "I'm going to the store and buy my own paint for the living room."

He looks at me indignantly. "My paint good."

"Sure it is," I tell him. "But I'm neurotic, I want my own."

I come back lugging five gallons of the best white paint. "No good," he tells me. I'm not sure whether his contempt is for the paint or for me.

"Maybe," I tell him. "But use it anyway, understand?"

"Okay, okay." Lighting the first of the cigarettes, he tosses the match on the floor.

I hover near him to make sure he does a good job. He's standing on the ladder, muscular arms reaching up to the ceiling. The tee shirt rises on his back; the skin is surprisingly white, fine black hairs rippling across it. Turning away abruptly, I go upstairs and stay there the rest of the day.

"What does it matter?" I say aloud after he's gone, as I stand in the echoing rooms. The downstairs walls and ceiling are snowy white, but who's going to come home and see them? The painting's thrown me back to zero.

But I can't afford to stay there, I've got to start putting all this stuff back. The blinds have to be rehung; my neighbors can look in on me, see how I'm stumbling around like a drunkard.

I used to wait for Mel to put them up. Well, it can't be *that* hard. I climb on a stepladder, forgetting to take the blind with me. Climb down, grab it, climb up again, tottering on the top rung. If I fall, will I be one of those pathetic old ladies with broken hips? I try to push the blind into place, but the piece of the frame that should swivel open is clogged with paint. I climb down again, grab the largest screwdriver, try to pry the frame open. A sharp twinge shoots through my shoulder, my old bursitis. Self-pity is waiting for me, crouching in the corner. Swinging the hammer full force at the frame, I narrowly miss smashing a windowpane. The blind pushes into place.

"I did it, Mel!" I shout.

Triumphantly I march over to the cartons of books to start putting them back on the shelves. I never realized how many of them are Mel's. I'd always thought of the books as belonging to both of us, all those poetry and play volumes. But there are some books on scientific theories that he was interested in the last few years. There's one that I gave him when he was ill that he never got around to reading. *CHAOS*, the jacket reads.

I collapse on the floor with the book in my lap.

The doorbell rings. It's Manny, generously offering to reconnect the stereo. I remember that he shares Mel's fascination with science.

"Here," I say, shoving the books into his arms. "For you. A gift."

"You don't have to do that," he says.

"Yes," I tell him. "I do."

32

Edie has cancer again.

"I'm going to live every moment that I have as fully as I can," she tells me. "There's so much to enjoy."

I'm terrified of losing this valiant friend who doesn't allow me to sink into self-pity because she doesn't tolerate it in herself.

"As we get older, life brings increasing losses," Joseph says when I tell him. "Mel won't be your last one. That's another reason why it's so important for you to be able to cope with his death." He looks away from me. "I've known losses, too." I know I'm not supposed to ask.

"It's so risky to let yourself care about anyone," I tell him. "One of my friends confided to me that she often contemplates suicide because she doesn't want to have to face the loss of people she loves. She said, 'I don't want all that pain.'"

"We all have a choice," Joseph says, "of retreating or loving. It's a risk for each of us.

"And we have the choice afterwards," he adds softly, "whether to give up, or to integrate our losses and go on."

I think about this new math of the older years, all these minus signs. I've always been afraid that people I love will leave me. I hate change. I want everything—everyone—I care about to stay the same forever.

The room is silent for a long time.

"I choose to risk," I say.

I heard that the Sioux Indians never say, "good-bye." There's no word for it in their language. But that doesn't stop the partings, does it?

"IT'S FUNNY in a way," I tell Joseph, "that now I think I have more capacity for love than I ever had before."

"That's a beautiful thought. Hold on to it."

"What good is it? I doubt there's going to be any love in my future."

"You talk about love as if it's just a man. But love can be other things: love of your children, your friends, creativity . . . Anne's love for Anne."

CANCER CARE gives us pamphlets titled GRIEF CYCLE. It looks like one of those children's board games, where you move from space to space. REAFFIRM is the last square.

"One will ultimately reaffirm the reality about oneself," it says. *"New strength . . . new self-esteem."*

It sounds good, but how do we get there?

The answer comes from a woman I meet in Ruben's waiting room, who confides that she was widowed years ago.

"How did you survive?" I ask.

"The first year was . . . the first year," she says, speaking the language we both understand. "It was only after I *accepted* his death that I was able to move on."

I tell Ruben what she said.

"Acceptance," he says, "will free all that energy you're investing in holding on to Mel and enable you to use it for other things."

Acceptance. What was, was; what is, *is?*

Can it really be that simple?

Of course, that isn't simple at all. Letting go is the hardest thing I've ever had to do.

During a vacation in Nantucket, Mel and I went on a walking tour past mansions built by sea captains in whaling days. On top of each house was a small roofed porch. "That's the widow's walk," the guide told us. "Sailors' wives used to keep watch up there, hoping against hope to see their husbands sail back into port."

We're all still waiting for them to come home.

THE GROUP wrestles with the GRIEF CYCLE.

"Can you see yourselves at REAFFIRM?" asks Nedda, pointing to the last square.

"I'm more at home in that square called PANIC," I say, trying to make it sound like a joke.

"I'm still stuck in the third one," says Henry. That's the square labeled DEPRESSION.

"How about the one called DRIFTING?" someone calls out.

Nedda looks around the table. "Don't any of you want to believe you're getting better?"

"It doesn't seem right . . ." a few voices begin and trail off.

"It feels like a betrayal of him," someone says.

We all nod.

But a stunning thought hits me: Isn't this denial of life a betrayal of *ourselves?*

IN RUBEN's waiting room there's a print of Van Gogh's *The Lovers.* A couple walking hand-in-hand along a tree-shaded path. I always avert my eyes from it, focusing on a spot on the wall or the brown metal of the air conditioner, anywhere but at those two people so close together.

"Look at Romeo and Juliet!" That's what a nurse called out when she saw us walking hand-in-hand up and down the corridors of Bellevue, while he was there for those drugs that didn't make any difference after all.

Today I sit down facing the picture and make myself look at it. I hold up one hand to block out the man. I wonder what direction the woman will walk in without him.

33

ONE PROBLEM WITH an ongoing support group is that people you become attached to "graduate," as Nedda puts it. Now it's Sandy who's leaving. How will we get along without her pithy comments? Each time someone leaves I feel another sense of loss. How do you ever make peace with this?

But new people keep coming in. We're getting more men, and they bring up different issues. What they seem mainly concerned about is finding replacements for their wives.

The women are blunt about how scant our chances are of finding someone. "Our bodies are aging," says Edna, "but our husbands always saw us as young as when we were first married." I think how blessedly myopic Mel was.

"I want to find a woman," admits Paul, that man who reminds me of Mel. "Maybe I'm too eager. I have to think about that."

"You sure lead with your head," says Muriel.

But there's another side to Paul. He confesses that for years he's been a "weekend artist." Now, he tells us, "I've given up my job so I can paint full time."

An artist, I think, how wonderful!

Maybe it's all this talk about relationships, but he seems more and more appealing. The attraction's obvious: he even looks a little like Mel. Tall, thin, very serious. Same tense face, hollow cheeks.

I find that I'm looking for him in the reception area, so we can have a few minutes of private conversation before the group begins.

"I applaud your decision to devote all your time to painting," I tell him.

"You don't think it's foolhardy?" he asks anxiously.

"Oh, no. I'm doing the same kind of thing, in a way. I'm a writer."

"So *you* know," he says, smiling at me.

One day he tells the group he's found a woman he can "relate to." I stare into my container of tea. If there were tea leaves in it, what would they read: give up?

The next week he's absent. Nedda's given all of us a list of each other's phone numbers. It's ten o'clock in the long evening of debating with myself before I'm able to dial his number. I phone from the room I work in; Mel's picture isn't on that wall. I hear Paul pick up the receiver.

"We" missed him this week, I say, is he all right? Yes, he had an appointment with a gallery, he's hoping to arrange for an exhibit. "That's wonderful," I tell him, breathing encouragement into the receiver.

"Frankly," he says, "I've had a rough week. That woman broke things off."

"You must feel terrible," I tell him, grinning at the phone.

But I run to Ruben frightened. How can I be feeling this way, Mel dead only fifteen months?

"This isn't anything pathological," Ruben tells me. "You're opening up to life."

"It makes me feel guilty about Mel."

"Mel's with God, what do *you* have?"

* * *

"Do WE have the right to be happy?" That's what comes up in the group now. Guilt's been placed on the table.

"I'd feel guilty if I saw another woman," says William, a shy man whose large spectacles frame eyes that look dazed. His wife's been dead for three months. He still sets her place at the dinner table each night. "A friend of my wife's invited me for coffee," he says indignantly. "How can a woman act that brazen?"

"It's only coffee," we tell him, laughing at ourselves as much as at him.

But a tall, stocky man who joined the group today looks at us mockingly. "I don't get this talk about guilt," says Victor. "To me, that's a coverup for other things. My wife and I had a lot of joy in our marriage, joy in sex. And I intend to pursue as much joy as I can."

"Good for you," says William nervously.

I'm jealous of Victor.

The following week I announce that I've been taking stock of the year. "I don't think I've made any major mistakes," I tell the group.

"Is a missed opportunity a mistake?" Victor asks.

I'm unable to answer.

He starts waiting for me after the group each week. I watch Paul, neatly dressed in a suit and tie, hurrying off to appointments. I go for coffee with Victor; sometimes I have drinks with Henry. I wonder if Paul notices how "popular" I am. I feel as if I'm in a second adolescence. I'm back on a diet. I'm running up my charge accounts buying new clothes. Bright colors. It's the first time since Mel died that I've cared what I look like.

In the group, Victor comments that most of the women are still wearing their wedding rings. "You'd think they'd take them off," he says. "Let men know they're available."

"Maybe we're not," says Muriel.

* * *

I TELL Joseph, "I feel that if I enjoy myself, I'm burying Mel."

"Mel's already buried. So what do you achieve by not moving on?"

"I don't know," I say, shredding my thousandth piece of Kleenex. "Even if I shut myself up in a room with my memories, I couldn't keep my marriage alive, could I?"

"All you'd keep alive would be an illusion," he says. "There isn't any marriage anymore."

So death ends the relationship, too.

The truth is, I'm not Mel's wife anymore.

I'M SITTING on the bed, staring at his picture, that face I'll never see again. How young he looks. One day I'll be older than he was when he died! I twist my ring around. It won't get past the knuckle. I go into the bathroom, soap my finger, sit on the bed watching him watching me as I twist the ring around and around, my finger turning blue. I work the ring over the knuckle; it slides down the rest of the way. I hold the ring in the palm of my hand, looking at Mel.

"With this ring," I tell him, "I thee unwed."

But I put it on my right hand.

34

THE UNVEILING'S ONE week away and the stone still isn't up. Am I going to repeat Muriel's awful experience?

I call Mr. Silverstone over and over again. And over and over again he assures me the stone will be there "in plenty of time."

Monday morning he calls to tell me it's at the stonecutters. "You can see it there if you want to."

His partner drives me to the stonecutter's shop. The monument's lying in the yard, turned on its side, wrapped in heavy plastic, wooden panels at the sides preventing me from seeing all of it.

The stonecutter's annoyed that I'm there. "I'll take off the wrappings if you insist," he says, scowling, "but it's your responsibility if the stone gets damaged."

"No, no," I tell him, "it's all right."

I'm down on my knees on the gravel, my head twisted sideways, trying to read. My finger traces the letters through the plastic to make sure each one is spelled right. What will I do if they're not? "Carved in stone" takes on real meaning! I read the words over and over, but they don't seem to register in my brain. Mr. Silverstone's partner drives me home, chatting about real estate as I stare through the windshield, surprised at how little I seem to be feeling.

But at home, anxiety returns full blast. Will the stone be up in time? Or will they forget, leave it in that dirty yard like a forgotten package? I call Mr. Silverstone again.

"I'm very tense," I tell him.

"I hear, I hear," he says.

I'm fretting about *every* aspect of the unveiling.

"My daughter's coming by car all the way from Massachusetts; what if she gets a flat tire on the way?" I ask the group. "My sister's driving hundreds of miles, she's always late. Suppose the weather's bad?" What if . . . what if?

They smile at me. "*You'll* be there, won't you?"

Henry just had his wife's unveiling. He surprises us by saying, "It marked a quiet reconciliation with myself."

"Just wear something bright," advises Helen, who's always practical.

Obediently I wash and iron a bright blue blouse.

There are only four days left.

That night I get a message from Mr. Silverstone. "You can relax, it's up."

The next morning I drive out to the cemetery. I need to see for myself.

And there it is. Looking just the way a tombstone should. All the decisions I agonized about, looking just right.

But as I walk around and around the stone, I glance at the husband-and-wife one beside Mel's, and panic. "A single stone is lonely," Norm had said. I've made the wrong choice! But then I remember that Mel always did like having some things just for himself.

I sit on the bench, staring at the monument. And the finality of it hits me full force. There it is, carved in stone, Mel Is Dead.

For the first time, I don't feel that he's here, knowing I'm visiting him. I have no sense of him being with me. That's more terrifying than anything else.

"Send me a sign," I whisper.

A single white butterfly skims past my face.

I GO from there to three restaurants to check them out for the luncheon after the unveiling; make a reservation at one where we can have a private room. It's the most expensive of the restaurants and I worry about that as I drive home, hearing Mel say, "Do you have to be so extravagant?"

But it's *my* decision, I tell him. I feel elated, imagining the luncheon scene. We'll celebrate Mel in anecdotes, raise our wineglasses in a toast to him.

The next day, reaction sets in; always that same pattern—insane high, suicidal low. I phone Joseph for help. He tells me my feelings aren't unusual. Nothing's "unusual," I think bitterly. He's trying to tell me that my anxieties aren't really about the unveiling.

"But it may rain."

"So you'll bring umbrellas."

And I hear him saying, "What's a ceremony? Just a cap. The real tribute is your love."

But this isn't what I want him to say. Tell me to come to see you, I plead silently, give me an extra session.

"I'll think of you on Sunday," he says.

Doesn't anyone understand that granite has replaced the sense of Mel being near me?

On Friday I do something I've rarely done: call the rabbi.

"I've officiated at numerous unveilings," he starts to say.

"Oh, I'm sorry, my brother-in-law is doing it," I say, nervously twisting the phone cord.

"Perfectly all right," the rabbi assures me. "What I wanted to say is that in my years of experience I've seen that the unveiling invariably brings a climax of feelings. But afterwards, there's usually a pacifying restfulness."

"A what?" I ask.

"It marks," he says, "the end of the *intensity* of mourning."

I'll buy that! So I tell myself that even if everything goes wrong—if everyone's late, if no one shows up at all, if the restaurant's disappointing. if it rains or snows (in June?)—I'll have a chance to, in Nedda's words, "find out how I can be strong."

SUNDAY MORNING I awaken from a few hours' sleep to see that the sun is shining. And I know that it's going to be all right; that for today, at least, God is in my corner.

David drives me to the cemetery; we laugh together in the car. Tamar's there already, everyone's on time, the sun continues to shine, the day isn't too hot. Norman officiates. The veil is lifted off a stone that everyone agrees is "beautiful." I read Mel's favorite passage from the Bible: *"A time to be born, a time to die . . ."* I stumble over the phrase *"a time to love . . ."*

Looking around at the gathering, I tell them, "If I could put one word on the stone that would sum up Mel, it would be 'Honorable.'

"The Honorable Mel Hosansky," I say, staring at the stone. "For me, that means he never willingly hurt anyone.

"I read somewhere that love is stronger than death. And I have learned this year that love *is* stronger," I tell them—and Mel. "I believe he knows about the caring and concern that have been shown to his children and me by all of you during these difficult months." (I avoid looking at Herb and Vella when I say that!)

"I'd like Mel's unveiling to have something that's not usually done," I say. "Please join hands, close your eyes, and send Mel a private thought."

Even the birds are silent as we stand there, hands clasped.

Then Norman leads us in the traditional prayer for the dead, the Kaddish. *"Yisgadal, v'yiskadash, sh'me rabbo . . ."* The syllables echo softly amid all those stones.

As we leave, each of us places a small pebble on top of the monument, the ritual to show that someone's been there.

I rest my hand on top of Mel's stone for a moment. It feels warm.

35

I MIGHT HAVE known: Back in the basement! Where is that fabled acceptance the unveiling was supposed to bring? I feel even worse than before; the unveiling was my last link with Mel, the last thing I could do for him.

I escape to my yoga center. "I'm in a state of crisis," I tell one of the leaders. He looks into the distance, thinking.

"In Greek," he tells me, " 'crisis' means a parting of the ways."

WHEN I get back, Victor calls. "What do you do in that place?" he asks.

"Get my head together, think about what I want to do with my life."

"You don't need to think. What you need is a love affair."

Is this a come-on? I'm not even sure.

"You're an attractive, vibrant woman," he says. "Don't turn your back on sexuality."

"I'm not," I say nervously. "It's just that anyone I got—involved—with, would have to be someone I cared about."

"That's old-fashioned. Just have joy."

I'm silent, twisting the cord around my finger.

"I guess we're not communicating," he says.

But I'm thinking what a long way I have to go to catch up with the 1990s. I feel like a female Rip Van Winkle waking up in a strange new world.

MY SESSIONS with Joseph are ending. Maybe that's also why I'm in such bad shape.

"It's natural to retrogress when counseling's coming to an end," he says.

I bring up the one thing I've been shy about discussing: my feelings about Paul. Will Joseph think I'm awful? But he, like Ruben, is beaming.

"Don't you see how healthy this is?"

"No," I tell him. "Anyway, it's futile. He never even asks me out. And I come from the generation that waited for the boy to do the asking, so I don't know how I could ask him."

"Risk!" says Joseph. "That's the way to unfreeze the future."

I'M HOME alone. Wandering around the house, I pick up Mel's copy of D.H. Lawrence's poems. Opening to a page at random, I read:

Grief, grief, I suppose and sufficient
Grief makes us free
To be faithless and faithful together
As we have to be.

I phone Paul. "I missed the group last week," I tell him. "How is . . . everyone?"

We talk about "everyone" for a long time. I mention that I'm hurt by something a friend said.

"It uses up too much energy to hold on to grudges," Paul says. Lecturing me. The way Mel used to.

"You're absolutely right," I say, delighted. He's lecturing; therefore, he cares. He'll fall in love with me, I'll be loved again.

Followed in a split second by that demon guilt that never stops hounding me. But didn't Mel say he wanted me to live "fully"? "Joyously"? Even marry again.

Paul's telling me he's going off in a new direction with his paintings. "More impressionistic."

I take a breath. "I'd love to see them."

There's barely a pause before I hear him asking if I'd like to come to his studio after the group this week.

"What a nice idea," I say, appropriately surprised.

But after I hang up, panic strikes. What will being alone with him in his studio mean?

Undressing to take a shower, I stare at myself in the mirror. My stomach's wrinkled, my breasts sag, my thighs are too heavy. My body's probably dead inside. Could I even respond? And how many people would be in the bed: *four*? His wife, my husband?

The day I'm to go to his studio, I pass by a large poster: "IF YOU MUST DO IT, DO IT WITH CONDOMS." I stare at it, not sure what I'm thinking; maybe, *catch up with the 1990s, lady.*

There's a drugstore facing the poster. I walk into it, like a sleepwalker.

"Need help?" asks the boy behind the front counter.

Shaking my head, I walk to the cosmetics counter, where there's a saleswoman. Leaning over, I whisper to her.

"Condoms?" she repeats in a voice that can be heard out on the street. "Down that aisle, honey."

I thought they'd be hidden away (I really am from another century!), but there's shelf after shelf of them prominently displayed. "Extra Strength," some say. This is premature to say the least, I tell myself. But I grab a box and hurry back to the saleslady. She sends me to that boy behind the cash register. He rings up my purchase with no more expression than if I were buying cough drops. Paying hastily, I hurry out of the store, run down the street, lean against a brick wall to catch my breath. "Crazy woman," I say out loud. A man stares at me. In a bathroom, I throw away the paper bag and hide the box under my make-up pouch. It shocks me—amuses me—that I'm walking into the bereavement group with condoms in my purse.

He dresses so conservatively, talks in such a measured voice, that I'm not prepared for the lushness of his paintings. "They're incredible," I tell him, staring at the abstract swirls of burnt orange, glorious turquoise, reds so vibrant they seem to enflame the canvas.

Delighted at my enthusiasm, he pulls out stack after stack of canvases. His back turned toward me is so like Mel's I dig my nails into my palm; he has the same bald spot on the back of his head that Mel had before chemotherapy. Some of these date back to his student days, Paul's explaining. I comment on his progress. Of course, I tell him, I'm not sophisticated about art. He assures me my comments are "extremely helpful." "Sensitive." "Perceptive." I'm drunk with power. "Dinner?" he asks.

We sit in a nearly empty restaurant; it's the evening before July 4th and the city is deserted. We talk for hours. His painting. My writing. His wife. My husband. Our mutual grief. Recovery. Love is never mentioned.

He tells me he's met several women, one who's only in her thirties, a "knockout." I keep the smile on my face. But he has a difficult time, he says, with the way these young women "blatantly" suggest . . . He doesn't finish the sentence, waving a courtly hand. What, he asks, has been my experience? Looking down at the tablecloth, I tell him there's "this man" (careful not to mention Victor by name) who told me I'm old-fashioned because I said that I'd have to care about the man. I draw curlicues on the cloth with my fork, hoping I'm playing this game well. "He told me that the idea is to just have fun." I look up at him. "Do *you* think I'm out of date?"

"No, no," he assures me. "I feel the same way. For me, it means commitment."

"Well," I say, worried I've gone too far, "commitment is a big word. It wouldn't have to be quite *that*."

The waiter comes with more wine. We talk of other things, laugh a lot. I haven't felt this joyous in longer than I can remember.

We make a date to spend July 4th together. He walks to the bus with me, holding my arm as we cross streets. I'm overwhelmed by the touch of his hand against my skin.

But home I look at Mel's picture and beg, "Bless me."

My God, I think in the middle of the night, what would my children say? But I've got to move beyond being Mama, too.

"If I were to get involved with someone," I write in my journal, "it wouldn't be that the man would be replacing Mel, but *supplementing* him." It feels good to believe this.

We have dinner together again the following week. (How differently waiters act when a woman comes in as part of a couple!) I tell him I'm thinking of going to the Metropolitan Museum Friday evening. He says he has a dinner date with a friend, but he'll try to break it and meet me. I sit taller in the chair, convinced I'm enchanting.

Walking me to the bus, past homeless people sleeping on benches, he comments how "disgusting" the scene is. His words upset me. I don't want to recognize the conventionality I've glimpsed in other remarks; don't want to see how much he isn't Mel.

At the bus stop, he kisses me good-bye in front of everyone. Cinderella sinks into a seat on the bus, grinning idiotically at the woman reflected in the window. She's wafted home in a coach that will probably turn back into a rotting hulk of a pumpkin, but at the moment it's a coach.

He phones to say he couldn't change his appointment. He doesn't sound regretful. "Perhaps next weekend." But his voice is cool.

"Why?" I keep asking myself. What did I do, what did I say? Should I have said yes, sex at any time, fun and games, let's be grown-ups? The singles scene is something I've never been trained for, am too old for.

I phone my friend Judy. Divorced, she's been dating for years. "Oh, babe," she sighs into the phone when I tell her about Paul. But I don't want sympathy, I want guidelines.

"You've got to find your own way," she tells me. "Trial and error, that's all you can do."

"I'll probably louse it up."

"That's all part of it, too."

"But I'm getting old. If it isn't this man, it will be no one, ever."

"Don't be ridiculous," she says, hanging up.

Then she calls back to ask, "Does it occur to you that he's probably scared, too?"

Against her advice to "cool it," I phone Paul a few days later. He seems glad to hear from me. "I picked up that book you wanted," he says.

"Are we on for this weekend?" I make myself ask.

"Yes. Saturday. Two o'clock. At the museum?"

He sounds as if he's making a business appointment.

By the time I meet him, I'm feeling rotten. He doesn't care about me, I know it. Maybe I sounded too straitlaced. Would it have been better to have indicated a willingness to go to bed with him? Or would eagerness be more likely to scare him away? And do I even want to? In the searing 98° heat, I'm wilted and weary. He leads me to the modern exhibit, explains what's "meaningful" in a canvas that's nothing but one straight line, like a slash of blood. But the glow is gone. I'm edgy and tired. What's wrong with me, I keep asking myself, am I afraid to let myself care? Or is it, I think, studying his profile, all fantasy, not someone I can love, just someone I'm trying to clone into Mel?

We go to a movie in the museum. "This is only my second movie," I remind him. "My heart's racing."

"You have to get over that."

"I will," I assure him.

In the darkness, he keeps his arms folded across his chest.

We have dinner together. He tells me he's leaving the group next week, then traveling for a while. "How wonderful," I say, ordering another drink. He drives me home. I invite him in for a "nightcap." We sit on the sofa; dear God, how incredible to have a man sitting here with me again. I've carefully sat down a few feet away. He would have to reach out to touch me, I'd have to reach . . . But our fingers stay clasped around the stems of our wineglasses. He criticizes the way one of my paintings is framed. The mini-lecture only leaves me weary this time. Want me, I'm thinking, no, don't . . . Put an arm around me, let me lean my head against your shoulder. He looks at his watch. It's 1:00 A.M. "I better leave," he says.

I don't disagree.

WITHOUT THE fantasy, I'm face-to-face with aloneness again. I think Paul doesn't want more than friendship with me. Maybe he isn't ready for more than that with anyone. Am *I*? A friend who saw us together tells me, "You were giving off vibes that you weren't ready."

But it's as if I've woken up. What am I supposed to do with these feelings? Numbness was easier. Now I know how needy I am. But it may never be. I may never be loved again, touched again.

It feels strange to be obsessed with a man, with life, after all these thousands of hours of grief and deadness. But I don't want my "success" to be measured by whether or not there's a man in my life. I've been working so hard to get a new sense of identity, I can't afford to lose it.

The problem is, freedom doesn't feel comfortable yet—like a new pair of shoes I have to get used to.

36

Nearly a year and a half. Finally, I'm able to take some memories out of the closet, even smile at them.

Walking in the country, I come upon a lake where people are rowing. We always used to row together on vacations in the mountains. "We" is the wrong word. I'd lean back lazily, trailing my fingers in the cool lake as I watched him enjoy rowing. It was the only way he felt secure around water.

He was afraid of canoes, because he'd once been alone in one and it had capsized. But he did go canoeing with me on a glacial lake in the Canadian Rockies. "I promise to rescue you," I said patronizingly. So ignorant I didn't realize no one could survive in that frigid water longer than a few minutes! We had sandwiches with us. Too hungry to wait for our picnic, I started munching on one. "You might share that," Mel said. But when I turned to hand it to him, the canoe rocked. "Don't move!" he shouted. So I put the sandwich on the end of the paddle and carefully lifted it toward him. "Send me back some of that soda," I said. And that's how we had lunch, "paddling" food to each other. I see us there, laughing on that sunlit ice-blue water, surrounded by towering snowcapped mountains . . .

You have to get used to being the only one left who remembers.

The pain still comes in waves—and some of them can be tidal—but they come less constantly. As Julie says, "The spaces *between* the downs are getting longer."

But you still have to be prepared to get hit unexpectedly. I'm on a bus going to meet a friend. The man across the aisle is reading a newspaper. As he holds it up, I see the sports headline on the back page, huge letters: MEL'S THE ONE.

You get used to bursting into tears in front of strangers. But you reapply the mascara, put the smile back on your face, go to meet your friend.

At a dinner party, the hostess seats me with another widow. She tells me, "It's been nine years and it doesn't get any better."

Panicky (it doesn't take much!), I phone someone who's been widowed almost that long. She tells me, "It's true the pain doesn't go away, but the smart thing is to build a life *around* it."

I tell Joseph I'm making a list of ways I can build around it.

"Read me your list," he says.

"Finishing this book I'm writing. Taking piano lessons. Recording for the blind. Teaching a writing workshop. Reading to hospitalized children. Tackling *Finnegan's Wake*. Traveling (maybe, at last, that trip to Italy?)."

"I hear progress."

"But it's all so sad. To move on, I mean. At first I couldn't stand being home at seven o'clock because that's when he used to come back from work. But sometimes in the past month I haven't even been aware it was seven."

"There's a saying," Joseph tells me. " 'Take what you can and leave the rest.' It's like what you told me about Paul. Even if nothing materializes from that, you discovered you still have the ability to laugh and to enjoy yourself. That's something to build on."

"I know Mel wouldn't want me to go around banging my head against the wall."

"No. And it wouldn't bring him back, either."

"No." The word sounds so final.

"Our sessions are coming to an end, too," he says. "So I'd like you to tell me how you think grief has changed you. What have you learned about yourself?"

I think about it for a few moments, while the fan stirs the humid summer air in his office.

"I guess," I say, "what surprises me the most is that I've been able to live alone. And I've been able to cope without leaning on anyone too much. I feel that I can take care of myself. I'm . . . how can I say it? . . . *stronger*."

"Wow!"

"Yes, that's a big wow, isn't it?

"How do you experience that strength?"

"As a kind of quietness I've never had before. I don't get as upset about every little thing. And I suppose—more of a sense of separateness. It used to be that I'd look at Mel's picture and think, why aren't you here? When are you coming back? But now it's as if there's more distance. I've had experiences he doesn't know about."

"I've never heard you use words like 'separate' and 'taking care of myself.' There's a kind of integrity in that. A stronger sense of identity."

"But I'm still so shaky, still don't feel it's really all right."

"You told me Mel wanted you to live fully. Tell him that you are, and that he'll always be a part of that."

"But it puts him more into the past."

Joseph looks at me.

"Maybe," I say, "it also puts me into the future."

"I hear progress."

I laugh. "Oh, Joseph, I'm going to miss hearing you say that."

"You have to say it to yourself." (I could have predicted that would be his answer.)

"I just wish," I tell him, "that Mel could have lived to see the grown-up I'm becoming."

NEDDA SAYS it's time to leave the bereavement group.

"The last thing I need is another parting," I tell her.

"You can't remain in kindergarten forever," she says.

On my last day, a new woman joins the group. She has the stunned face of the newly widowed. Hearing that voice of someone lost in the woods, I realize how far the rest of us have come. Almost without realizing it, we've managed to reach—as Nedda puts it—"a different place."

The new woman looks at us wistfully. "Does it get easier?" she asks.

"No," I tell her, "but you get stronger."

MEL'S BIRTHDAY again. The July 16th that devastated me when I read it on the milk carton.

David calls to tell me about a dream. "Daddy was a candle flickering," he says. "I kept putting my hands around it, telling him not to go out. But he went out anyway. It was so frustrating."

I take that beautiful dream to Joseph at our final session.

"You're a candle, too," he tells me. "Put your hands around *your* light."

He walks me down the corridor, gives me a farewell hug.

"Burn brightly," he says.

EPILOGUE

THREE YEARS.

I made our trip to Italy. By myself, in September. First I took some Italian lessons. "Tell me the word for widow," I asked the teacher. *Vedova* I wrote inside the cover of my phrase book.

In Rome I stayed in a hotel alone for the first time, but Cousin Ruth was only a few blocks away. The first few nights we ate supper in her apartment overlooking tile rooftops and tiny terraces with trees blooming on them.

The fourth evening she wasn't well and asked to be excused from dinner. "I'm a big girl," I said, "I don't have to have someone with me." But that familiar panic was choking me. I'll skip dinner, I thought, grab a slice of pizza from a stand. Distracted, I slammed the iron gate of her courtyard—forgetting to take my thumb out of the way. For six months afterwards the nail was a blackened souvenir of Rome. Angry at the pain— and my childishness—I dared myself to go into a restaurant. Walking to the nearby Piazza Navona, I found an expensive-looking cafe. The *maître d'* looked around to see where my escort was. *"Uno,"* I said in a voice that was much firmer than I felt. Seated at a table—the only person alone—I thought everyone must be staring at me. But hadn't Ruth once said that she'd found nobody cares? (Or is that worse?) I twirled my wineglass, playing the role of famous American author choosing to dine in solitary splendor. A little girl came to my table selling flowers. I bought a rose and asked her (proud of my paltry Italian) what her name was, her age. Miraculously, she understood me. I left the waiter a lavish tip and nodded regally as he bowed. Safely outside, I grinned triumphantly at strangers sitting by the fountains.

Rome was a schizophrenic experience. One part of me so high on the incomparable art and ancient ruins; the other aware every minute of the one who wasn't there. Everywhere I went I seemed to be the only woman who wasn't either with a tour group or holding someone's hand. When I asked directions of a group of nuns, one of them said in English, "But you're not traveling *alone*, are you?" Tired of being made to feel like an oddity, I snapped that my husband was dead. Easier to say that terrible word in Italian, *morto, morto.* "He is with you in spirit," she assured me.

But his invisible presence wasn't enough on my birthday. Needing to feel close to him, I went to a place I knew he'd have wanted to see, the house where Keats had died. In the faraway days of our youth, Mel helped me with my term paper about Keats's heartbreaking letters to his lost love. In one of the rooms I found myself face-to-face with Keats's death mask. It looked like Mel. I ran out in tears, hearing Mel reciting the words he'd courted me with: *"Arise my love and fearless be . . ."* All the thrill of the trip ebbed out of me. What good was it without him?

That night I met a man. A friend of Ruth's, an English actor playing small roles in Italian films. Ruth had suggested we join him and his wife for capuccinos after dinner. He arrived alone; his wife had to work. He looked like Michael Caine. Sitting at the small table as if he owned the entire piazza, he asked in a bored voice how I was enjoying Rome. "I have a love/hate relationship with this city," I told him. He gave me an interested look. "I do, too," he said. We exchanged loves (Michelangelo's *Moses*, Etruscan museum, ruins by moonlight) and hates (traffic, traffic, traffic). "I don't know why I worried about the plane," I said. "Crossing the streets here with all those motorcycles is much more dangerous." He said, "But you, I'm sure, know how to cope with danger." The conversation switched to his work and how few roles were available these days. I sympathized, I said, having been an actress. He swiveled toward me as though he'd found a kindred spirit, and we exchanged stories about the profession we both loved. After a while Ruth said she was tired, but why didn't he show me Rome at night?

He led me along the Tiber, told me legends about the antique sculptured heads on one of the bridges. Pulling me closer for a "better view," he gestured toward the dome of St. Peter's in the distance. But I was looking at the gold band on his finger.

We strolled around that illuminated city—it had never seemed so luminous alone—until after midnight. He said Ruth had told him about my "situation" and he'd been afraid I'd be morbid. But I had such "serenity," he said. Serenity! I laughed. "You're certainly a spirited woman," he said, holding my arm tighter. I felt "spirited"—and young. I belonged with those couples walking arm-in-arm. He said he'd escort me back to my hotel. Heading back, I felt so shaky I could barely hear him. As we reached the entrance, I turned to him uncertainly . . .

At that moment the lobby door opened and a young girl came out, a newly minted Venus in form-fitting jeans and an abbreviated top that showed her unwrinkled midriff. A jaunty cap perched on her curls. She took out a cigarette. "Do you have the light?" she asked, with a charming accent. Quickly he pulled out a silver lighter, cupped his hands around the flame as he leaned toward her. "Where are you from, dear?" he asked. "Holland. With my class. So boring." He held her wrist to help her steady her cigarette. "You're far too lovely to be bored for long," he said. She glanced at me, back to him and giggled, then hurried away with all the hopefulness of youth. I suddenly felt unbearably weary.

"Good night," I said. "Thanks for the guided tour."

"Perhaps we'll meet again."

"I'm leaving for Florence in the morning."

"What a pity," he said. "You won't have a chance to meet my wife."

ARRIVING AT the *pensione* in Florence, I realized I was in a city where I didn't know a soul. Shown to my small room, I tried not to feel that familiar panic. "Time to be a grown-up," I reminded myself. I went to the terrace for a glass of wine. Two American women were sitting there talking. They invited me to join them. "I'm a widow," I confided, "making the trip my husband and I were supposed to have together." I waited for sympathy. "Aren't we all?" said one of the women briskly. It seems they were both widows, traveling together. I had dinner with them. "We always eat in the *pensione*," they said. "You never know how safe it is outside with those gypsies." Afterwards I said I wanted to see Florence. They insisted on accompanying me. And there it all was—the massive Duomo looking like painted cardboard in the moonlight, the enormous arms of the Uffizi, the Arno shimmering with upside-down reflections of quaint buildings on the Ponte Vecchio . . . The excitement I thought I'd lost in Rome swept over me.

I discovered that there could be advantages to being in museums by myself, taking time for what *I* wanted to see. To wander though medieval streets and browse in colorful markets at *my* pace. Most evenings I ate in the "safety" of the *pensione* with my new friends, but sometimes I chose to eat alone, in an outdoor cafe in the stagelike setting of the Piazza Della Signoria, surrounded by colossal statues—and inevitable musicians singing romantic songs. I would fantasize Mel sitting in the vacant chair on the other side of the table, lift my glass as though in a mutual toast. Back home, friends had warned me that Italy is "for lovers." But isn't the whole world? What are you supposed to do, leave for another planet?

The last afternoon in Florence I went to the Bargello. Across a gallery, a bronze statue drew me like a magnet. Donatello's *David*. Not the confident hero that Michelangelo created, but a young boy, his foot on the slain giant, the eyes saying, "Well, I've done it, but what is next for me?" Awed at his new power . . . and a little uncertain.

IF MEL were to return, he'd be surprised at how I've changed. Sometimes *I* hardly recognize myself. I came back from Italy stronger. In moments when I feel terribly alone, I remind myself how I coped in a foreign land.

Mel thought the hardest thing for me would be living alone, but lately there are evenings when I prefer to be by myself; to write, read, listen to music. I still talk to him, but not as often. When I need his advice, I find myself answering aloud with the words he'd use. I know so well how he'd react to everything, so in that way he's still with me. Trying to sleep, I find myself rubbing two fingers over my forehead, and remember that was his gesture.

My wedding ring is stored in the safe-deposit box.

"How are you doing?" we, the bereaved, ask each other. The answer is invariably the same: "Up and down." You keep busy with whatever involves you in *life*. These days I'm chairing a fund-raising group for Cancer Care, and I've been asked to speak to audiences of newly widowed—as if I'm some kind of role model! It makes me feel powerful. That's a brand-new feeling.

"Hey, but listen," I tell friends, "I still haven't been to a movie alone." ("You could go to Italy by yourself and you can't go to a *movie*?")

We each have our individual monsters.

But I will. When I'm ready.

That still remains the password. "When you're ready," we keep assuring each other.

When I'm ready. . . . What if that man in Rome hadn't been married? What if that girl hadn't come through the door? I think now that when, if, the "right" man comes along, I'll be ready to love again. But I'm working on not needing to be linked to someone in order to feel complete. That woman who used to be married to Mel seems like a child in many ways. *"Baby doll."* That was Mel's pet name for me. You have to say good-bye to the person you were, too.

I'm grateful for all those years when I was so well-loved and cared for. But if I never am again, there's still so much else in life. Work. My children. Friends. Travel—a whole world to see yet. It is, after all, a good century in which to be a woman.

IN THE support group Sandy said, "Since we grew at different rates as children, isn't it understandable that we're healing at different rates?" There's no set time for all of us to reach certain goals, and some things some of us may never reach. But this is what it means to be *this* widow after three years—and for you, somewhere along the same road . . .

> You introduce yourself without saying in the next breath, "I've lost my husband."

> When you get a phone call asking for him, you're able to say, "He's dead."

> You're still sleeping on one side of the bed.

> You can tell amusing stories about him—and laugh.

> You're familiar with the tool kit!

> You read a book he'd have enjoyed or hear gossip he'd have relished . . . and can't share.

> You can be home alone without feeling that someone is missing.

When you talk to him you no longer expect him to answer.

It still hurts to see couples holding hands.

You automatically say "I" instead of "we"; "me" instead of "us."

You stay up reading as late as you wish, make dates without checking with anyone, come home whatever hour you please.

You give yourself permission to be attracted to other men.

You still love him.

During Mel's illness I burst out with that universal question, "Why us?"

"That's just the way it is, baby," he said.